24 JAN 2023

KINGS
FOR A DAY

Hailing from Dromintee at the foot of Slieve Gullion in County Armagh, Niall McCoy is a writer, journalist and sports enthusiast. He has worked for RTÉ, the *Irish News* and *Gaelic Life*, and is a regular contributor to other media outlets.

A life-long Armagh fan thanks to the influence of his father Desy and uncles, Niall has followed the highs and lows of his beloved Orchard County, and is looking forward to their second All-Ireland win.

KINGS
FOR A DAY

**The Story of Armagh and their 2002
Journey to Sam Maguire**

Niall McCoy

THE O'BRIEN PRESS
DUBLIN

First published 2022 by The O'Brien Press Ltd,
12 Terenure Road East, Rathgar, Dublin 6, D06 HD27, Ireland.
Tel: +353 1 4923333; Fax: +353 1 4922777
E-mail: books@obrien.ie Website: obrien.ie
The O'Brien Press is a member of Publishing Ireland.

ISBN: 978-1-78849-298-0
Text © Niall McCoy 2022
The moral rights of the author have been asserted.
Editing, typesetting, layout, design © The O'Brien Press Ltd

Pictures Sportsfile.
Cover and internal design by Emma Byrne.

8 7 6 5 4 3 2 1
25 24 23 22

Printed and bound by Scandbook AB, Sweden.
The paper in this book is produced using pulp from managed forests.

Published in

DUBLIN
UNESCO
City of Literature

Contents

Prologue - Unscrewing the Cap   page 7

Chapter One - Ulster Says Go   10

Chapter Two - The Two Brians   18

Chapter Three - Orchard Blossom   38

Chapter Four - The Hoodoo   62

Chapter Five - Tribal Warfare   87

Chapter Six - More Than a Game   102

Chapter Seven - Lourdes or La Manga   122

Chapter Eight - Marching Towards the Sam   134

Chapter Nine - Conquering the Hill   157

Chapter Ten - Thine is the Kingdom   173

Chapter Eleven - A Red Hand Rivalry   196

Chapter Twelve - The Pursuit of Greatness   218

Epilogue - The Little Gold One   235

Prologue

Unscrewing the Cap

In 1953, after Armagh defeated Roscommon to reach the All-Ireland final for the first time ever, the Orchard management booked out Tommy Mackle's Hotel in Maghery for a pre-final training camp.

Short of space to room the players, beds were instead lined out in the main hall. For days, the players shared the space with couples celebrating their wedding breakfasts.

Everywhere they travelled in the small village on the edge of Lough Neagh, starry-eyed youngsters followed. These included Kevin Rafferty, who would go on to play in an All-Ireland final some 24 years later.

Twenty special trains were put on for the meeting of Armagh and Kerry at Croke Park, half of these coming from the northern direction, with starting points such as Clones, Monaghan, Portadown, Enniskillen and Derry. Over 150 special buses were booked through the Ulster Transport Authority.

The attendance on final day was officially registered at 85,155, but with fans streaming in through open gates at the Canal End, 92,000 or so was a more realistic estimate. It seemed the entire county had decamped to Dublin, as Kerry supporters were outnumbered five to one. A sea of orange and white was ready to celebrate their crowning moment.

No team from the six counties had reached an All-Ireland final since the controversial establishment of Northern Ireland in 1921. The occasion was embraced with wild enthusiasm. The result, however, was not.

Armagh returned from Dublin crushed. Bill McCorry entered sporting folklore for all the wrong reasons, thanks to a 54th-minute penalty miss. If converted, it would have put the Ulster side a point ahead; instead, the Kingdom ultimately ran out winners 0-13 to 1-6.

'We'll get it next year.' They didn't. Instead, Peter McDermott, the referee who had awarded the penalty that McCorry drove a yard wide of the post, captained Meath to the All-Ireland title in 1954. Then another year passed, and another, hope slipping away with each advancing season.

When Armagh finally made it back to the September showpiece in 1977, a bottle of whiskey was put behind the counter in McKeever's bar in Portadown. Jameson Redbreast, 12 years old.

The whiskey, their victory dance, sat patiently as the days counted down to the team's game against the mighty Dublin. However, those Sam Maguire dreams would again be shattered.

Paddy Moriarty joined McCorry in missing an All-Ireland final penalty for Armagh, but that error mattered little as Dublin steamrolled the Ulster champions.

The whiskey wouldn't be opened to provide solace. 'Leave it until we do win the All-Ireland; it'll not be long.' Next season maybe.

Back into the shadows the bottle went, waiting, almost forgotten, regulars wondering would its contents ever be poured and savoured as they should. As the years – the decades – went by, the bottle's dust cover grew thick.

On Tuesday, 24 September 2002, two days after Oisín McConville had joined McCorry and Moriarty in missing a penalty for the Orchard County in the All-Ireland final, the Armagh squad were handed a glass each. The dust was blown off the whiskey bottle; the cap was unscrewed.

Chapter One

Ulster Says Go

The 1991 Ulster Championship started with a bang – literally – for Down's new great white hope, James McCartan.

The future two-time Mourne County manager was at home the night before Down were due to face Armagh, who he would come close to joining just a few years later, in a provincial quarter-final in Newry when a 600lb IRA bomb exploded in Donacloney.

Instead of much-needed rest, McCartan worked through the night, sweeping up glass in the family pub and providing shelter for neighbours who had been displaced.

Less explosive was the clash in Newry between the bitter rivals. The horrendous encounter was matched only by the conditions and Armagh's Jim McConville falling over himself with the goal gaping. His miss allowed Pete McGrath's men to sneak through with two points to spare.

Much as many old hands in the border town push the boundaries of truth by claiming they were at U2's famous town hall concert in 1980 – booked by Mickey Magill, father of future Down All-Star Miceal – a number of fans have claimed they were the source of the famed quote shouted as the crowds dispersed from the Marshes that day:

'The pick of those two teams wouldn't win an All-Ireland ...'

That story still airs every so often, all these years on, the scorn in the sentiment barely softening with time.

In September 1994, Armagh stars Jarlath Burns and Kieran McGeeney – known to most as Geezer – squared up to each other in training, coming close to blows.

Their moods had been simmering for years as continuous unfulfilled dreams drained their devotion. Meanwhile, neighbours, footballing enemies, had their cravings sated.

The pick of those teams in '91 wasn't meant to win an All-Ireland, but Down would embark on a wondrous journey culminating in an All-Ireland final win over Meath.

The following year, the Donegal players scaled the Hogan Stand steps to lift the Sam Maguire Cup for the first time, and northwest neighbours Derry dutifully followed their lead in 1993.

'Watching other teams going on and winning All-Irelands from Ulster was great, but it was a bit annoying too – "could we not do that?" "Why can we not do that?" says Joe Kernan, who was Armagh's assistant manager under Paddy Moriarty from 1989 until that rain-soaked day in the Marshes in 1991.

'There wasn't much between us, but in fairness to Derry, Down and Donegal, they were three great teams.'

Down were about to underline that greatness. In early September 1994, on the night that Burns and McGeeney lost their cool, Down were also training. There was a tension in the air there too, a whiff of cordite ready to explode. In Armagh, frustration was the potential accelerant. For Pete McGrath's side, anticipation.

Orchard County boss Jim McCorry had decided to bring the squad in early to get ready for October's National League opener against Mayo. A few miles down the road, the Mourne County were preparing for an All-Ireland final with Dublin.

Some of the Armagh players had to drive through roads bedecked in black and red on their way to training – a constant, unwelcome reminder of where Down stood, and how far Armagh had to go.

Orchard coach John Morrison had set up a simple sprinting drill. Player A stood on the 45-metre line and Player B stood five yards behind. Burns and McGeeney were paired together and when the whistle sounded, the former took off for goal with ball in hand.

Like a lion hunting a gazelle, McGeeney chased his prey down and dragged him down coarsely from behind.

'Fuck me, Geezer,' roared an angry Burns, 'that's a foul and a booking.'

McGeeney shot back, questioning Burns's masculinity, and a shoving match broke out. The pair were separated, but silence provided the soundtrack for their car journey back to south Armagh together. Those red-and-black flags fluttered provocatively once more as they came through Newry and steered towards country terrain.

Goalkeeper Benny Tierney, a club-mate of McGeeney, had quelled the rising temperature between the pair with a few jokes. The Mullaghbawn man was mercifully armed with the wit to defuse many a sticky situation.

Inside, though, he was hurting as much as anyone. The goalkeeper had been called into the Armagh panel for a McKenna Cup game by Father Sean Hegarty when he was still a student at St Colman's in Newry. He joined the squad properly in the late 1980s. Through his bright white smile, Tierney's teeth would grind as an endless run of Ulster sides, Armagh not included, enjoyed their day in the sun.

Unable to see a way to end Armagh's sorry sequence, his own strategy was to ensure he was as good as he possibly could be – the constant appraisal of Tierney's jovial demeanour far too easily overlooked a fierce competitive streak.

'I took over from Brian McAlinden, who was probably the most celebrated goalkeeper in Armagh's history, at 19 or 20 years of age, and that to me was an honour,' says Tierney. 'I always wanted to be number one; I always believed that I was number one. Now, I could meet a thousand people out of a thousand and twenty and they would tell me that I wasn't number one, but in my head I was.

'You have to believe in yourself and you have to believe that you're good enough. I don't know where that came from. Boys would tell you that when they're playing golf with me for a pound, I'll hole a putt for 30 foot on the last hole and I'll say to them, "It's not because I'm competitive," and they'll say, "No, it is, you're totally competitive." That's in you.

'You see anyone that's walking up the steps to lift an All-Ireland or a club championship, be that junior or senior or intermediate, they have to have that competitive will and that drive, and they have to realise that you have to give something up for that as well.

'You're not living the life of a monk or anything like that, but there has to be a time where you have to settle down and try and be the best that you can be.'

A few weeks after Burns and McGeeney had been on the brink, Down defeated Dublin in the All-Ireland final. Ulster everywhere, Armagh nowhere – on the surface, at least.

The early 1990s belonged to other counties in Ireland's northern province, but building blocks were being put in place that would ultimately provide the most solid of foundations for their momentous 2002 Sam Maguire success.

It can be traced all the way back to that horrible 1991 day in Newry, when Mickey Linden sent Tierney the wrong way from the penalty spot for what would prove to be the match-winning goal.

Before that tasteless main, the Armagh minor team had slammed home six goals against Down in a sizzling starter course. Des Mackin scored a hat-trick, while Barry O'Hagan dominated at midfield. Their teamsheet also included goalkeeper Darren Whitmarsh and Pat McGibbon.

The former would play in front of 30,000 fans at Old Trafford the next year as a Manchester United side featuring Paul Scholes, David Beckham and the Neville brothers faced Leeds in the Youth Cup final. In 1995, McGibbon would also play at the Theatre of Dreams alongside Beckham and Eric Cantona as Alex Ferguson's side suffered a shock League Cup loss to York City.

Whitmarsh was still in goals for the Armagh minors in 1992 when they got agonisingly close to an All-Ireland crown. Leading by two points a couple of minutes into additional time, Trevor Giles – destined for a glorious career in the green and gold of Meath – played the ball into Royal substitute Michael Farrelly. With his marker Kevin O'Hagan slipping on the turf, the Kells man blasted beyond Whitmarsh.

Barry O'Hagan was presented with a chance to equalise from a '45', but, against the wind, it dropped short. Though the ball was flicked onto the crossbar, the full-time whistle had already sounded.

That tormenting experience was crucial though. Many of the players from that team remained close to manager Brother Larry Ennis until his death in 2021, particularly Paul McGrane. The coaching received from Liam McCorry was also banked and called on for years to come.

Two years later, the Orchard minors were back on the All-Ireland stage after claiming another Ulster title. In that 1994 clash at Croke Park, the class of 2002 would again be represented, with Aidan O'Rourke, Enda McNulty, John McEntee, Barry Duffy and Tony McEntee – listed as Anthony in the match programme – in the first 15.

It was Kerry who ended their hopes then, Armagh's dream dying in the last four.

'Mike Frank Russell and Kerry beat us in the semi-final in Croke Park,' says Aidan O'Rourke. 'That minor team could and should have won an All-Ireland, but we didn't have the belief that we could do that.'

Sigerson football was also providing a launchpad for expectation, with legendary college coaches such as Jordanstown's Adrian McGuckin, Jim McKeever of St Mary's and Queen's Dessie Ryan having a massive impact on some future Armagh stars.

There had been highlights before – Ger Houlahan won the Player of the Tournament award in 1986 as Jordanstown won the colleges' title, and John Rafferty collected the accolade three years later when St Mary's prevailed. Benny Tierney was goalkeeper for the Ranch, the moniker of St Mary's in 1989.

In the 1993 season, when Queen's defeated St Mary's in the final, Armagh's power-packed potential was there for all to see. Kieran McGeeney,

Andrew McCann, Cathal O'Rourke and Paul McGrane were all key members of that QUB team.

On 22 September 2002, 12 members of the Armagh squad that arrived at Croke Park for the All-Ireland final against Kerry had tasted success at Sigerson level with various universities. At the media night before the game, Queen's coach, and a former Tyrone selector, Dessie Ryan made a presentation to Armagh captain Kieran McGeeney to recognise the county's contribution to the Malone Road institution. Geezer received the memento on behalf of the 13 panellists who had played at Queen's.

'Dessie's training sessions were notorious. You could be on the training pitch two and a half, three hours on a Wednesday, and at stages of the session you'd be fucking froze, because he'd stand for 20 minutes and explain why you don't put your foot there when you're turning; this is why you step; the man is a genius,' O'Rourke continued.

'We would have rehearsed, repeated, rehearsed, repeated – repetition, repetition, repetition. I bring a lot of that into my own coaching now. That just builds into people's muscle memory. I know what he is going to do; I can see the flight of this ball before it's kicked; I know where to move and when. Dessie would drill that into the Queen's boys and that was crucial for how we played for Armagh.

'Joe Kernan's tactics were very similar with and without the ball and I benefited from Dessie's coaching because I already had what Joe wanted from his wing-backs.

'What Joe did was give us a simple, workable plan that didn't need a lot of elaboration. The ball went into the forward line a certain way and it went early.

'If people had asked at that time about my strengths, no one would have said I was a brilliant kick passer. I developed as a kick passer in 2001, '02 and '03 because Dessie Ryan wanted that strategy, the diagonal ball to the back post.'

Even at schools' level, future stars were making their mark. Diarmaid Marsden, who would become perhaps the most idolised Orchard player inside the four dressing room walls by that 2002 group, starred as St Colman's won a Hogan Cup in 1993.

Two years earlier, Kieran Hughes had won a MacRory Cup with St Pat's, Dungannon, against a St Colman's side containing Marsden and Paul McGrane on the same day as Barry O'Hagan took home a MacLarnon Cup title with St Michael's, Lurgan.

When Down captain DJ Kane lifted the Sam Maguire in 1994, ideas of an Armagh challenge looked more fanciful than ever. Below the surface, however, the roots were taking hold.

Chapter Two

The Two Brians

The Armagh players, bodies jaded and in some cases very bruised, filed past the officials, political representatives and members of the clergy sitting on the side of a trailer. The footballers made their way into the makeshift changing rooms after the day's club action.

It was standard procedure for a Sunday in the mid-'90s. Play a club League game in the afternoon, hop in the car and then play for your county that evening at an official pitch opening. The location of the second match generally determined whether or not you had time for a shower in between games.

Club football in the Orchard County was renowned for its physicality – an unquantifiable badge of honour, no doubt manufactured on a pub stool, which proclaimed Armagh and Meath as the hardiest in the land. The validity of that particular assertion can be debated, but it was no place for the faint-hearted. Punches flew, hits were frequent and there was enough testosterone on show to alert an Olympic drug tester.

On that particular Sunday afternoon, a brawl had broken out between two clubs towards the north of the county. The referee took the unusual step of abandoning the game rather than waiting for the participants to run out of steam.

Two of Armagh's noted hard men were involved. It was particularly vicious, and the acrimony remained. One of the unfortunate quirks of an abandoned match is that it doesn't give the two teams the opportunity to shake hands at the end of the game and say 'no hard feelings'.

In the Armagh dressing room later that evening, this bad blood led to a confrontation between the pair. An offer to step outside from one was instantly accepted by the other, and the antagonists headed for the door to pick up where they had left off earlier.

Some quick-thinking players and coaches realised that the sight of two Armagh players taking lumps out of each other in front of the Archbishop probably wouldn't lend itself to positive headlines. The pair were dragged back inside the changing room and through a mesh of bodies they got a few shoves and half-punches in. Enough for both to feel that they had stood their ground, anyway. The fact that they were teammates mattered little in that moment.

Those types of cracks were all too obvious in the Armagh dressing room in the early 1990s, splits that hampered the work of manager Jim McCorry and his assistant John Morrison. When Brian McAlinden and Brian Canavan replaced McCorry as Armagh manager in late 1995, those fissures in the Orchard core were still rotting away.

'That sort of only stopped around 1998,' says former Armagh captain

Jarlath Burns. 'Paul McGrane and Diarmaid Marsden and these boys started talking about Club Armagh. That term, Club Armagh, resonated, and we made a decision that whatever happens at club level had no business with what went on at county level.

'The best way to deal with those rivalries was through humour, and the best person to deal with that was Benny Tierney. Benny is a joker, but Benny Tierney is indispensable within the dynamics of a panel. He creates levity when levity is required.

'Within a panel, things can become very tense, particularly coming up to a championship match when a starting team is emerging. You can see who they fancy, who they want, just by what they're trying and the line-outs they're putting together in training. That becomes very evident.

'You always need someone in the changing room to cut the tension from that.

'From St Colman's to Mullaghbawn to Armagh, he has won everything, apart from an All-Ireland Club. Armagh didn't win an All-Ireland after him; the dressing room would have been more serious. Benny Tierney was a man that just continually broke the tension.'

For Tierney, who played midfield for his club right up to U21 level, being the class clown came naturally.

'When I look at the players now who are hooked on phones and social media, they're coming out of training and the first thing they're going looking for is their phone,' says Tierney. 'The first thing we were looking was to see what prank we could pull on each other, see what we were going to do or mess about with somebody and have a bit of a laugh.'

Such capers were commonplace in the Armagh squad in the mid- to late 1990s, especially on weekends away. They could be as simple and as immature as filling an unsuspecting player's bag full of kettles, or as downright annoying as the approach taken by Justin McNulty.

The Mullaghbawn man had taken to ringing his teammates from his hotel room and reading passages of the Bible to them. The phone would usually be hung up on the other end before it was discovered whether or not the Romans ever wrote back to St Paul.

In 1999, on the day before Armagh's All-Ireland semi-final meeting with Meath, McNulty was doing his ring-around when physio Dan Turley answered. Thinking it was hotel service, Turley listened intently until McNulty got bored. That evening, the player was at Turley's table for dinner when he remarked how attentive the hotel staff were to do such a thing. McNulty nearly fell off his chair.

Those lighter moments are fondly remembered now, but when Brian McAlinden and Brian Canavan called the first team meeting as joint-managers, they knew it was a dressing room not short on inner tension.

Canavan, referred to as Barney by those who know him best, says that they planned to get around some of it by way of familiarity.

'There were better players in the county that weren't on the pitch. It might have only been one or two, but it can make a difference. We felt that having a man from the north, mid and south would cover all bases.

'We'd know all the players between us, and it wouldn't be hard to pick up a phone. I could ring someone from Dromintee or Crossmaglen or Silverbridge for a chat about anything, because they'd know me from south Armagh. Brian would know the Clan na nGael lads and all those well, whereas I wouldn't have been as close.

'It worked fine, because by the time we got to 1999, we had the best players on the panel. Between rows and ructions and everything else that goes on, for those couple of years we had the best players there.'

Those rows were tolerated, because they were working with a united dressing room. That anger and frustration was often welcomed, as long as everyone was pointing in the same direction, that being to bring Armagh football forward.

'I remember one night in Lurgan. Enda McNulty was marking me and he ripped the bib off me and I swung for him,' Oisín McConville recalls. 'Aidan O'Rourke came in and swung for me and Cathal O'Rourke came in and swung for Aidan. That was a sign that things were flipped – I knew we were going to be alright after that.'

That unity hadn't been there when the two Brians took up the reins.

To understand the dynamic of the partnership, you need look no further than the interview process from a few weeks beforehand.

Canavan inadvertently put himself into the frame during Armagh's 1995 Ulster Championship clash with Derry. He took aim at Armagh whilst on BBC media duty.

The Oakleafers, still smouldering from their early exit to Down 12 months previously, arrived at the Athletic Grounds determined to show they were still All-Ireland contenders – despite the war that had broken out in the county following the unexpected sacking of Eamonn Coleman.

Even with the fallout from that move simmering throughout 1995, Derry – now led by Coleman's former right-hand man Mickey Moran – delivered the goods. The half-back line of Johnny McGurk, Henry Downey and Fergal McCusker enjoyed the freedom of the Cathedral City to provide the launchpad for a 1-17 to 0-10 trimming.

It stung some of the players more than others.

Cathal O'Rourke had stroked over seven frees across the game, but was in a foul mood when speaking to the press afterwards.

'We trained approximately 470 hours for this game. That's for one hour's football. We let ourselves down; we let our county down; we let our families down. I know the feeling of depression that's going to be with us now, and it'll be with us for a long time. I know because we've had it before so often.'

Armagh player John Grimley didn't hold back either. Taking aim at the management team of Jim McCorry and John Morrison, the 6'4" powerhouse said that he would be stepping away and that his twin brother Mark would be doing likewise. This was an acrimonious end for players who had represented their country in international rules in Australia.

An unfortunate end too for McCorry, who had won a Dr McKenna Cup and had taken the side on a memorable run to the 1994 National League final.

In another part of the ground after that heavy Derry loss, the knife was also being twisted, via a radio microphone, by Brian Canavan, who had captained the Orchard County five years previously.

Canavan's words were noted by members of the County Board. One official went to meet him to pick his brains on how Armagh football could move forward. That conversation evolved into a temperature check on his potential availability.

The initial interest was there, but Canavan also put forward Brian McAlinden's name. The pair hadn't been especially close as players, but Canavan had never played with anyone who had displayed more footballing intelligence than the Sarsfields man.

Enthused by the idea, Armagh asked the pair to attend an interview. McAlinden, as old school as they come, declined. 'If they want us, they can give us it,' was his thinking. Canavan, more willing to play the game, went and represented the pair of them. The good cop/bad cop routine would be a trademark of their tenure.

Walking into the interview, Canavan met another contender, a certain Eamonn Coleman, disposed of by Derry so controversially. In the meeting with officials, Canavan revealed that it was not just a joint ticket they were proposing, but a triple threat, also including Grange man Peter Rafferty.

'I said we needed Peter Rafferty for the mid-Armagh boys,' Canavan said. 'Peter was a good fella and had started to take teams. He was one who jumped out at me.

'Armagh arranged a meeting between the three of us and, long story short, the three of us decided that we'd take it on. Unfortunately, in the end, Peter wasn't able to, so Brian and myself took it on.'

First impressions cannot be underestimated and the two Brians made a good one on a cold October day in 1995.

Distinguished former players making their inter-county managerial debuts would typically make plenty of headlines in the weekend newspapers, but the press focus was on two other men in similar circumstances.

Páidí Ó Sé, an eight-time Celtic Cross winner, had been handed the task of awakening his native Kerry from their slumber, while three-time Dublin All-Star Barney Rock was preparing for his first game as Westmeath boss.

The two greats endured mixed fortunes. Kildare came to Tralee and turned over Kerry, while in Newcastle, Westmeath defender Dermot Brady shut down new Down captain Mickey Linden to ensure that Rock's reign got off to the perfect start.

The focus on events in Drogheda was less intense, but satisfying still for the new management, as Armagh started with a 1-14 to 0-8 win over Louth. The goal came from that most familiar of sources, Ger Houlahan, while Diarmaid Marsden's transition to senior football continued to prove almost unfairly easy.

A defeat of All-Ireland champions Dublin, albeit minus eight of their All-Ireland winning 15, was another early boost, although a dislocated shoulder for prolific scorer Cathal O'Rourke was a real sour note.

Armagh were also without Marsden, Kieran McGeeney – who had hurt his shoulder in Mullaghbawn's Ulster Club win over Castleblayney – and Paul McGrane, meaning that Andy McCann was handed his debut, Justin McNulty doing likewise a week earlier against Louth. The seeds for 2002 were already being sown.

Those two wins ensured that the League objective of Division Two safety had been all but achieved by Christmas, and Armagh ended up coming very close to promotion, only to miss out on a potential play-off when they fell to a Colin Corkery-inspired Cork in the final round.

McAlinden and Canavan hadn't taken the job merely to earn promotion though. They came in to make the Orchard what it had been in their heyday – a feared Championship outfit.

Facing a hotly fancied Derry in 1996, this time at Celtic Park, was the perfect means to measure any improvement a year down the track.

McAlinden, in particular, would bristle at any suggestion that they were there simply to make up the numbers. When they raced into a four-point lead after eight minutes, the shock of the summer looked on the cards.

Jarlath Burns had been imperious in those opening 20 minutes, and that domination owed a lot to some mental kidology from McAlinden.

'We warmed up in in St Columb's College before the game in Celtic Park,' he said. 'Jarlath had a problem, a ligament problem in his ankle.

I asked him would he take an injection to help with the pain, and he said he would.

'I rang the doctor as he was coming to the match and I explained about the ligament. When we got to the College, he said it's too late, it won't work.

'I told him to give him an injection but put nothing in the needle. Jarlath got an injection with nothing in the needle. Half an hour later, I asked him how he was feeling. "Brilliant, absolutely brilliant." He was cured by an injection with nothing in it.

'I told him that story one day, and he just shook his head.'

Brian Mullins's side would eventually take control when Joe Brolly plundered a goal early in the second half. Full-time: Derry 1-13 Armagh 1-6 and another campaign had fizzled out.

The start of the 1997 season was a proud one for Benny and Bernadette O'Rourke and Sean and Geraldine Duffy. Three years earlier, their sons Aidan O'Rourke and Barry Duffy had jumped on a bus at the Carrickdale Hotel with a group of lads. They stood on the Canal End as a sea of orange took over Croke Park for the National League final against Meath.

Big days were to be savoured back then for Armagh fans. Although Meath ruthlessly swatted them aside, the lukewarm tins and the craic around the ground sweetened the pill of defeat.

Those Armagh fans also loved a pitch invasion, something evident in spectacular fashion when their 2002 awakening arrived.

O'Rourke and Duffy were among those who ended up on the field after that Meath game, looking around at a stadium that resembled a construction site at the time, as the old Cusack Stand had been bulldozed months before.

Three months later, the pair would be back on the pitch, playing this time, as a fancied Armagh lost an All-Ireland Minor semi-final to Kerry.

Like nine of the players on the 2002 Armagh squad, including fellow 1994 minors Enda McNulty, John McEntee and Tony McEntee, they had been learning their trade at the Abbey CBS in Newry. The '02 alma mater also hosted Cathal O'Rourke, Justin McNulty, Kieran McGeeney and Oisín McConville. Manager Joe Kernan also received his education at the Abbey.

Prior to the 2002 final, the ten headed back up Courtney Hill for a photo with school principal Dermot McGovern. Also included was Val Kane, who was vice-principal at the time.

Kane is a famous name in Down football. Val was part of the 1968 All-Ireland winning squad and also won an Ulster title in the 1980s as part of a joint-manager ticket alongside James McCartan Snr. His brother DJ captained the Mourne County to the Sam Maguire in 1994. Three years earlier, DJ Kane had marked one of his students, Cathal O'Rourke, in the 1991 Ulster Championship clash between Down and Armagh at the Marshes.

Val Kane may have been a revered figure in Down, but he also played a major role in Armagh's rejuvenation.

'Val is old-school, but he is a trained PE teacher and aware of what others were doing. He would have been a big man for basketball and bringing patterns and habits from that into your game. We would have played a lot of basketball in the Abbey at the time,' Aidan O'Rourke says.

'That had a big influence on my game. When it became a thing to video games and watch back for learning purposes, I remember thinking: that's basketball. Some of the moves I didn't even realise I did, they came straight from basketball.

'Val was the first person to ever introduce us to anything close to strength and conditioning. Now, they were fairly basic programmes, but it was about the ethic. You go to the gym twice a week and you do your session, and you were in charge of making sure that the other boys were there too.

'As a seventh year, I would have had responsibility for sixth and fifth years to make sure they were there, and all that. Character building, leadership development, work ethic to do the session – that was all very important.

'Kilbroney Park, the park around the school, mental stuff. Psychologically in terms of resilience – dig in and find more – I think that was massive.'

The bonds were forming, and as those same pupils progressed to college in Belfast, digs were shared as life took on a different look. That preparation in the gym meant that they adapted to college football instantly, dominating physically. Enda McNulty and the twin McEntees were quickly called into the Armagh senior team after that 1994 minor season.

At the start of the 1997 season, the two Brians decided to call in some more former county minors, including Aidan O'Rourke and Barry Duffy. County secretary Paddy Óg Nugent phoned the student house to ask the pair to training, but, it being a Monday night, it was drinking time.

As the lads sank pints in Renshaws, a female housemate was scribbling a note to pin up on the fridge for the boys.

'Barry and Aidan to go to Armagh training, 7pm tomorrow, Davitt Park.'

After closing time, the group headed back to the house for an afterparty. It was in full swing when the note was noticed.

'Fuck, you have to go,' insisted Enda McNulty to the pair. 'You have to go.' At that moment though, finding beers in the fridge was the top priority.

The next morning, the phone rang and rang again. Nugent delivered the details for a second time when the phone was eventually lifted.

The two lads, hardly fit to move, made it to Lurgan that night and just about survived one of McAlinden's famous vomit-inducing sessions.

McAlinden was in foul form that night, ahead of their third National League match against Monaghan at the start of December.

It had initially been postponed due to the weather, and they'd been told that the game would be replayed on 12 December. Instead, it was brought forward a fortnight to form a double header with Crossmaglen's Ulster Club clash with Bellaghy. Two games on one pitch in the winter was a recipe for disaster, McAlinden felt, especially with his players featuring in both matches.

O'Rourke and Duffy were expecting an easy first day as Armagh players. A 12.45pm throw-in meant they'd be up the road to Belfast in great time after taking in the match from the bench. They were only among the substitutes because of a glut of injuries anyway.

However, with the Crossmaglen contingent absent and a minor car crash en route to Clones ruling out a few more players, Duffy and O'Rourke were unexpectedly thrown in from the start.

News reached their parents, whose chests swelled with pride, but as the ball was thrown in, they couldn't see the boys. Other Armagh fans were bewildered too. Duffy, not unlike Ivan Drago from the Rocky films with his bright blonde hair and unmistakable presence, was a hugely exciting minor and there was plenty of anticipation about what he could add to the mix.

Those blonde locks were missing though. Doing what students do in the lead up to Christmas, they had gone drinking and with it came the inevitable bad decisions. In this case, it was taking a Gillette razor to the head and a shave right down to the scalp.

So two players, with just a few days' growth on their heads, made their Armagh debuts with nobody able to recognise them. Their parents eventually worked it out, and they were left happy too. O'Rourke, playing corner-forward, hit a goal in the 21st minute, and Paul McGrane added a second a minute later. Duffy got a point as well in the 2-9 to 0-8 win.

Armagh would finish mid-table in Division Two when the 1996–97 National League came to a close. Their seven games had brought two wins, two losses and three draws.

Down or Tyrone would provide the Ulster Championship opposition. As management was still unsatisfied with the team's conditioning, a training weekend was organised. The venue was Thurles, and that word is still enough to send a shudder through anyone involved in the 1997 panel.

'Jim McCorry believed in looking after players, in the sense that if we went away for a weekend, we stayed in a bloody good hotel,' Jarlath Burns remarked. 'Brian McAlinden did not believe that: "These boys are soft, we have to harden them up." McAlinden was right. We were soft-centered.'

As the bus rolled towards the Tipperary town, the players wondered which hotel they'd be staying in. But on the journey went, past hotels and B&Bs, until it pulled up at the town's seminary. Opposition fans always did say that Armagh would need some divine intervention if they were ever to win an All-Ireland.

More used to chocolates on the pillows on these weekends away, the players were far from pleased. The mood worsened when they were told they were heading to Thurles Racecourse to complete five laps.

The grass was long and wet, and the 30-odd men panting as they did laps of the course, with McAlinden barking out orders, would have made for an unusual sight for any equine enthusiast who happened to be in the vicinity.

Back at the seminary later, word filtered through that Hayes Hotel, where the GAA was formed in a billiards room in 1884, was within striking distance. Some of the younger players planned a visit that night, not for a history tour but for the disco that was taking place.

Management got wind of this and McAlinden stood up after dinner to tell the squad that if anyone attended, the whole squad would be heading to Thurles on Sunday morning, this time for seven laps of the racecourse.

Team captain Jarlath Burns pleaded with his troops, 'Not tonight, lads. Please, just this one night.'

A few hours later, Burns got a knock at his door and was summoned to meet the management. On his way he clapped eyes on one sheepish-looking player who had been caught trying to escape through a window.

Others had avoided detection and were dancing away in Hayes Hotel. The perfect crime it was not, however – as the four laughed over pints, four eyes were on them: those of Brian McAlinden and Brian Canavan.

At breakfast the next morning, management told the players to stand up and admit their crime. To the surprise of the two Brians, five rather than four players confessed. With one more body than expected, McAlinden brought them back to the racecourse, while the rest of the panel got a few hours of downtime.

'I had a bottle of water which I was drinking out of,' says McAlinden. 'One of them asked me for a drink, and what was left in the bottle I poured out into the grass and said, "There's none left." Another one of the boys said, "Don't ask him; I'd die with thirst before I'd take it off him."

'That was the relationship we had, but it bore its fruits when we got the victories in Clones.'

McAlinden had wanted to send the entire squad back to the racecourse as punishment, but Burns pleaded with him. 'I said, if five boys come into my class and they don't have their homework done, I don't punish the whole class, I punish the five boys,' recalls Burns. 'I'll never forget McAlinden's reply. He said, "Can you not see the difference? Five men miss their homework, five people miss their homework. But if four people fuck up in the first round of the Championship, we lose. Everyone loses."'

The Sarsfields man listened to his captain though, a surprise to Burns. The one player whose advice McAlinden would occasionally heed was defender Colm Hanratty, a hugely respected figure in the Armagh dressing room.

That goes a long way to explaining the reaction to the broken leg suffered by Hanratty in a 1997 National League clash with Donegal in Lurgan. Even goalkeeper Benny Tierney was admonished in the press for his angry behaviour, perhaps the one and only time in his career that had happened.

Even in the middle of a row, Tierney could make people laugh, as Peter Canavan had found out a few years earlier.

Back in 1989, Armagh and Tyrone players had brawled in the corridors of Healy Park at half-time of their Ulster Championship clash. It was legendary amongst the two panels for its viciousness.

'The referee, Michael Greenan, called Brian McAlinden, the Armagh captain, and the Tyrone captain out at the start of the second half and said that the first person that lifted his hand was going to the line,' said Paddy Moriarty, who was Armagh manager at the time.

'Almost from the throw-in, someone in a white jersey ran in and milled Mark Grimley in the back of the neck. The referee couldn't have missed it, because it was at the actual throw-in, but he didn't do a thing about it.

'It practically took Grimley out of the game and he was playing some stuff. They went on and won the Ulster Championship.'

A few months later, the teams were drawn together at the Castleblayney tournament in Monaghan. Effectively a set of challenge games, Armagh and Tyrone would face off in the Paddy Cole Cup semi-final on Sunday, 12 November. Monaghan and Cavan would meet in the other last-four clash the following Tuesday.

This was the first time the sides had crossed paths since the 'Battle of Healy Park' and, with no threat of suspension, old scores were there to be settled. Armagh had led at the break, but Tyrone took control after the interval to win 2-14 to 0-8. When referee Danny Lee sounded the full-time whistle, all hell broke loose as 27 players tore into each other in brutal fashion.

Three players opted not to engage. A youthful Peter Canavan was being marked by his cousin Leo McGeary and, with Christmas just around the corner, they chose to avoid any potential awkwardness at the family gathering.

As he watched the savagery, from behind Canavan heard, 'Come on, Canavan, ya wee bollocks, I'll bate ya.' Turning around to see what awaited him, Canavan was met with the sight of Benny Tierney, a friend from St Mary's Training College in Belfast, laughing and calling him in for a sham fight.

Now, eight years later, Tierney was beside himself with rage as things spiralled out of control against Donegal.

The clash between Hanratty and Donegal player Shane Bradley produced accusations and counter-claims and, inevitably, violence. The sound of the leg break was clearly perceptible to those close to the pitch, and caused many stomachs to churn.

'There was enough electric undercurrent to fuel the national grid,' Philip Reid wrote in the *Irish Times*.

Donegal manager Declan Bonner took his players into a huddle on the pitch as Hanratty was being treated, and that prompted Brian McAlinden to make a beeline for Jarlath Burns.

'McAlinden came on and said, "Are you going to let those boys have a talk on our fucking pitch?" I said, "What do you want me to do?" "Get into the middle of them; this is your pitch."

'I went into the middle on my own and the row started again. "Get the fuck out of here!" "I'm going nowhere." Juvenile stuff – a fully qualified teacher at this nonsense.

'Cormac McGill, father of Fergal McGill from Croke Park, wrote in his match report that "Jarlath Burns, who spends his summers in the Donegal Gaeltacht, walked into the middle of the Donegal team and promised them a watery grave." I laughed out loud when someone sent that to me.'

Donegal had video footage of the incident and were horrified at the accusations thrown at their player. Eamonn O'Hara, writing in the Irish News, had described it as 'a wicked and indefensible act', prompting the Donegal County Board to release a statement condemning the paper's coverage of the incident.

That was the second time McAlinden had raced onto the field to confront Burns. The first had been a few months earlier, during the 1997 Ulster clash with Tyrone.

That fitness work in Thurles had been banked and Armagh entered the game fully confident of progressing. Anticipation was growing as the Enniskillen Band started to play and the teams headed over for the pre-match parade.

Burns was feeling extremely relaxed and led his team into position along the perimeter wall on the terrace side. Tyrone captain Peter Canavan came over to tell him he was standing behind the Tyrone flag and to move.

At an Ulster Championship match in 2014, Armagh captain Ciaran McKeever stood behind the Cavan flag and as he saw the Breffni players approaching, he turned around to the man behind him in the line-up, goalkeeper Philip McEvoy, and said, 'We're not fucking moving.'

McEvoy didn't, nor did the players down the line, and when the Cavan players barged into them all hell broke loose. Key Cavan forward Martin Dunne missed the game with a suspected broken hand, allegedly sustained in a punch thrown at Jamie Clarke. Armagh won the game.

Seventeen years earlier, when told by Canavan to move, Burns realised his mistake and did exactly that – to the absolute disgust of McAlinden.

'I saw McAlinden coming on and I though he was going to take me by the throat,' said Burns. '"What the fuck are you at? Are you going to let Peter Canavan do that to you?" I said I was behind the wrong flag. "It doesn't fucking matter; it doesn't fucking matter." He gutted me.'

That wasn't the only issue stoking the Tyrone fires. Earlier in the week, ahead of his Ulster debut, Oisín McConville had done an interview and afterwards made a few disparaging remarks about the Red Hand full-back line, believing the on-the-record portion of the conversation had ended.

'I was asked off the record and I was naïve. I was 19, 20 years of age. Adrian Cush ran up to the top end of the field and said to the boys, "Did you see what he said about you this morning?" I had no idea what was in the paper; it was only afterwards when I got home that I saw it. It wasn't something that stopped me doing interviews, but I was just a bit more guarded.

'I think I kicked eight points and I had eight or nine wides. Maybe eight misses, a couple into the 'keeper's hands.

'We'd no chance to rectify it. Not one person in that changing room said one thing to me. I didn't socialise with the boys; I came home and gathered my thoughts and was back playing club football within a week. You move on.'

Those remarks didn't cost Armagh the game though – the 18 wides clocked up over the 70 minutes did that. McConville was guilty of a number of those and, at a stage when he was missing frees, people were questioning why he was in the team at all.

The player remembers being totally blotted out by Clare's only football All-Star in a November 1994 draw and another point gained as they shared the spoils with Cork four months after that match.

'I remember playing Clare in Division Three. I was marking a guy called Seamus Clancy and he just ate me up and spat me out.

'We played Cork in 1995 then and Jim, my brother, was injured – the ambulance actually had to come onto the field and take him away after a bad tackle. We had a 45-yard free and Jim sat up on the stretcher and he said, "Make sure you fucking kick that, because I've been killed for it."'

McConville did land that free to rescue a point, but in Omagh against Tyrone his radar was off.

Armagh threw it away. Jarlath Burns, Kieran McGeeney and Paul McGrane were destroying their opponents around the middle. When Chris Lawn was sent off in the 51st minute for a high challenge on Martin Toye, the momentum had swung, especially when John Rafferty broke forward for an inspirational point moments later to move the visitors ahead.

But the match was lost – or won, depending on your allegiances – three minutes from time when Jody Gormley broke down the flank and looped an effort goalwards. Justin McNulty was well positioned to cut it out, but a shove from Mattie McGleenan sent him forwards with the Eglish man slapping the ball past Tierney to the net. Replays showed a clear foul, but Pat McEnaney was happy to continue and Armagh's season was over. The Monaghan whistler could have provided a scapegoat, but the reality was that Armagh had lost the game, nobody else. All they were left with was another drive home filled with regret and disappointment.

However, all of that paled into insignificance later that night, when more serious news filtered through. Tyrone minor Paul McGirr had died, after an accidental collision in the minor match with Armagh goalkeeper Willie McSorley as the Red Hand player scored a goal.

As McGirr was being treated on the pitch, Armagh were in Dromore for their pre-match warm-up. Jarlath Burns always made a point of grabbing a chat with the volunteer who had stayed behind at these grounds to open up, allowing others to head to the game instead.

'Have you anyone playing in the minors?' he asked.

'We've a lad McGirr; I think he's just got a goal ...'

Chapter Three

Orchard Blossom

On 14 June 1998, Armagh recorded their first Championship victory since a preliminary round win over Fermanagh back in 1994.

Jim McCorry's side had reached the National League final earlier that season, but they had failed to bring that fearlessness into Ulster. The side needed a fine showing from the late Kieran McGurk and a goal from Ger Houlahan to fend off the Erne County.

A young Peter Canavan tore them to shreds in the next round to secure a win for Tyrone in Omagh. Defeats to Derry in 1995 and 1996, then the Red Hands again in 1997, would further test supporters' patience.

The wait finally ended in 1998, kick-starting the county's love affair with sunny days in Clones.

For the next decade, the streets around St Tiernach's Park would regularly fill with orange jerseys, though not all locals were enthused by the Armagh invasion.

As buses filled with young people from all over the county converged on the Monaghan town, the famed 'Buckfast Brigade' was born. While there is no doubt that the lure of pints attracted some to Clones as much as the football on show, they were very much the minority. The colour, passion and support the Armagh faithful brought to these occasions would take on a life of its own, instantly assaulting the senses in what was fast becoming Armagh's home away from home.

When they met Down in June 1998 in the Ulster quarter-final at Clones, Armagh fans outnumbered Mourne County supporters considerably. As was tradition, the victory was followed by a pitch invasion – and the celebrations were merited.

Armagh led by just a single point early in the second half when Enda McNulty picked up a second yellow card. At that stage, fans feared the worst, especially with Paul McGrane and Jarlath Burns losing the midfield battle to Greg McCartan and Sean Ward up until that point.

Brian Canavan had been positioned high up in the stand for a better viewpoint, but the tension proved too much and he made his way down to the sideline as the game appeared to be slipping away from his troops.

But the character that would define this team emerged over the next 30 minutes.

Kieran McGeeney, named at centre half-forward but taking up position in the number six berth, was sensational. Justin McNulty blotted out Ross Carr, while Diarmaid Marsden, despite missing a 13-metre free early in the second half, was starting to cause mayhem. Crucially, Burns and McGrane began to win ball in midfield.

Marsden and Ger Houlahan, who had replaced Cathal O'Rourke, started popping over the points. Paddy McKeever, who sat an A-Level

English Literature exam the next morning, was excellent on his championship debut. When Benny Tierney denied Shane Mulholland's snapshot, the die was cast.

Armagh won 0-16 to 0-11, sparking wild celebrations amongst the majority of the 24,300 present.

Speaking afterwards, team captain Burns was clearly taken aback by the character shown when the odds were against his team.

'I have played on good Armagh teams beaten by Down teams that were not as good as us. We were beaten because we carried so much psychological baggage with us. We simply psyched ourselves out of it.'

Armagh were dreaming – a first Ulster final appearance since 1990 was suddenly within their grasp. Old adversaries Derry stood in their way in the semi-final.

Big days call for big moves, and Armagh goalkeeper Benny Tierney now decided to debut one of his famed patterned jerseys. In grey and black, the design looked like the result of someone playing Tetris after 12 pints. It was just one of a number of memorable tops that the Mullaghbawn shot-stopper would produce over the years, in a nod to famed Mexican soccer goalkeeper Jorge Campos.

'They called me Compost rather than Campos,' smiles Tierney.

'O'Neills sent out one of these paint explosion jerseys and Brian McAlinden threw it in the bag – he wasn't going to let anyone wear it. I fished it out of the bag and wore it one day, and it got remarked upon, and I suppose it fitted in with my childish personality.

'And then O'Neills saw me wearing it, so they started sending me more of them, I think for their branding. McAlinden didn't care; there was one luminous one and McAlinden actually said that four opposition players turned straight away and looked up at the glare of it. I suppose I wore it because I just liked a bit of colour.

'I've given them all away over the years. It was different, and sometimes you have to embrace your weirdness. If every school principal was the same, if every pupil was the same, if every footballer was the same, there'd be nothing. You have to embrace your weirdness and just get on with it.

'The jersey meant nothing to me when someone was bearing down on goal. It was just something different.'

With the crowd at fever pitch, Armagh were on level terms with five minutes to go. The game, history for this team, was at their fingertips.

Those old cracks started to appear though. The Orchard County wouldn't score again, while Derry added 1-4 to their tally. Ten players who would start the 2002 All-Ireland final were among the first 15 that day. Talent was not a problem; Armagh were simply unreliable in the big moments.

'In 1998, there was a sense going into the Down game that they were old and we were coming. We put them away and there was a feeling that we had arrived, but Derry were on the horizon,' says Aidan O'Rourke.

'Derry were a completely different challenge, and I'm not sure there was enough belief that the job could be done. They were so seasoned at that stage. Anthony Tohill was still at the height of his powers, Henry Downey was a rock at centre half-back and they were bringing in a younger batch, the likes of Enda Muldoon. They were formidable.'

Brian McAlinden left Clones that day with unshakable doubts about his attack. They had wilted when the game was there to be won, while Derry had embraced the challenge when the gauntlet was laid down.

He yearned for the kind of shrewd operator who could stand up in those big moments and it almost came in the most unexpected of forms.

A few months after the Oakleaf defeat, a form would be signed that ultimately prevented McAlinden from pulling off one of the most controversial GAA transfers of all time, which would have seen a darling of Down football, James McCartan, pulling on an Armagh jersey.

In November 1998, the two-time Down All-Ireland winner at last transferred clubs from Tullylish to Burren, following a drawn-out and, at times, messy affair.

Bumps along the road prevented McAlinden from getting McCartan's transfer from Down to Armagh over the line a couple of years later. It would have been a Celtic to Rangers-level move, and the fallout would have been huge amongst supporters, but the transfer application went into the Ulster Council regardless.

'Some of the County Board officials weren't overly happy about it, but we didn't care. We just wanted victory and to get silverware,' says McAlinden.

The provincial body ultimately turned down McCartan's desired move, on the basis that his literal place of birth – Craigavon Area Hospital – was not enough to qualify him for the Orchard County.

If McCartan and Armagh were to push further, the only option that appeared open was for the player to transfer clubs again, this time into Armagh, with Ballyhegan a rumoured destination. Given the drama of his previous move to Burren, that was never a serious option.

'Put it like this: I was asked and I was interested, because Down had made it clear that they weren't interested, because they wanted to turn over a new leaf,' said McCartan of the potential move.

'Once I knew the Down story, that there was no chance of a new chapter for me, I was asked, and everyone wants to be wanted. Once it was pointed out to me that I would have to change clubs to do it, and it probably took me a while to win people over in Burren and be accepted, I wasn't going to turn round and move clubs again.

'Even though the lure of playing inter-county football was there again, I wasn't going to do that. It was a big decision; I had to go through a lot to get the Burren transfer over the line, so I didn't want to go through that again.

'The opportunity was there, but as I say, it's the biggest positive thing in Armagh that James McCartan didn't go and play for Armagh. Could you imagine if Armagh won the All-Ireland and I was playing? You would have gotten no credit whatsoever. The Down people would have had it over you: "They couldn't win it with their own team – they needed to get a Down man in!"'

McAlinden had been on a team holiday in Thailand, and waited patiently for Paddy Óg Nugent's phone call to reveal the outcome. As disappointed as he was, the Orchard County's attacking options looked a lot more promising in 2001 – when McCartan's proposed transfer was up for the debate – than they had done after that Derry defeat in 1998.

On a freezing day in Ballybofey in November 1998, the same month that McCartan made his move to Burren, Armagh had experienced their own change in direction.

Their trip to Donegal had started in unusual circumstances. The management had called for a players' vote on their captain on the morning of the game. Jarlath Burns had led the team out for two seasons and his reaction was one of relief. The Silverbridge stalwart had already decided that this would be his final year with the team, so a season focusing solely on his football appealed greatly.

Being captain of your county is an extraordinary honour; it also comes at a heavy cost to your time. Burns lifted his pen and didn't have to think twice about the name he was going to scribble down – Kieran McGeeney.

In the dressing room before the game, Brian McAlinden announced that the votes had been tallied and their captain for the season would be Jarlath Burns.

Burns had to take a few seconds to process the news. When a players' vote is called to decide a captain, it is with a change in mind. Shock soon turned to anger for the big midfielder. His position had been clearly undermined and while he did phone McAlinden that night to tell him as much, events after the vote that day tempered the ferocity of his reaction.

The first round of National League fixtures that season carried extra intrigue, as the GAA's Football Development Committee was trialling some experimental rules. Goalkeepers, when in possession, were now not allowed to play the ball with their hand. Yellow and red cards were introduced, in place of a referee taking notes for first offences and pointing to the line for the second.

Donegal were severely weakened by injuries, so much so that manager Declan Bonner had to forgo the usual practice of naming his team days before the game.

Armagh were also down players, as their Crossmaglen contingent were not involved with the panel at that time. They had been due to play Antrim champions St John's in the Ulster Club semi-final the week before, but it was postponed until the week after the Donegal game.

Despite that, Armagh were excellent for ten minutes, nabbing the opening two scores. From there though, they were outscored 1-10 to 0-4. The home side eased across the line, with the Orchard players visibly giving up long before the full-time whistle.

They trudged back to the changing room and the door was slammed shut. It would not open again for a few hours, as players and management tore into each other.

All issues thrown onto the table, and high up the list was a brewing tension between Armagh and Crossmaglen. The Rangers had been crowned All-Ireland champions in 1997, but the following season they had lost to Errigal Ciaran at the Ulster semi-final stage.

Joe Kernan's men were determined to regain their crown and the manager wanted his county contingent to focus on club commitments. The Armagh management wanted access to the same players.

In recent times, parties involved have tried to deflate that particular political football but it caused genuine strain. An uneasy truce usually held, and no nuclear option was activated. Oisín McConville felt he could have served two masters, and also believes that better dialogue would have helped keep a lid on things.

'In the changing room after the Donegal game, we were the topic of conversation. It was about us not being available,' says McConville. 'A lot of the guys I played with would disagree, but I do think that is something that could have been sorted with management. A deal made along the way. There seemed to be a lot of vested interest at the time, and it wasn't ideal us coming in after 17 March in those years.

'At that time, I didn't care if we won a League game or not with Armagh; even towards the end of my career it wasn't that important. You wanted to play Division One, because the best teams were there, but it was all for Championship.

'I didn't think missing out on a few League games mattered that much, but the boys felt differently. When we came in, a boy that had played four or five games might have had to step aside for us if management decided.'

Crossmaglen was not the only issue on the table. In a heated debate, fingers were pointed and players were asked if they were honestly giving their all. Did Armagh believe they could win Ulster? It was hot and heavy, but it was cathartic.

The dynamic of the Orchard dressing room was peculiar. Elder statesmen like Jarlath Burns and John Rafferty, in particular, were highly respected, but Kieran McGeeney and Paul McGrane, some years younger, were the two dominant forces inside those four walls.

Less vocal but leading by example was Diarmaid Marsden. The very idea of McGeeney idolising another player seems outlandish, but he was in awe of the Clan na nGael powerhouse. Everyone was.

'Geezer, Floppy (McGrane) – you couldn't have put an Armagh team on the pitch at that stage without those two,' says Aidan O'Rourke. 'They were kids in their twenties, but they were well established. They had big days, carrying their team and going toe-to-toe with the best players in the country.

'Kieran McGurk, Marty Toye, players like that were coming towards the end of their time; that was obvious to everyone. Now, older players are important in any culture – they set standards, drive the thing on, they add experience. I would never discount the importance of that.

'Jarlath would have been part of that older generation, and John Raff. They were the epitome of using their experience, nurturing their younger players. Both were key. When I see articles in the paper about Joe or Jimmy being 33 and how it's time to move on, I always think of the influence of Raff and Jarlath on those teams. Older players get discarded too quickly.'

When the dressing room door finally opened and the players walked into the cold November air, something had been ignited inside the panel. Now it was time to follow it up with action.

Their next match was a home game against Dublin, and Armagh were much improved.

Jim Gavin and Declan Darcy, his right-hand man on the line, have won multiple Sam Maguires for Dublin in recent times, and years earlier in 1998 their excellent free-taking had earned their county a draw when Armagh had been the better team.

The Ulster men then had one match left pre-Christmas – the long journey out west to face reigning All-Ireland champions Galway.

'We beat them,' says Jarlath Burns, 'and that was the day we won Ulster.'

Galway manager John O'Mahony visited the Armagh dressing room after the 3-9 to 1-11 win, to commend them on the aggression and work-rate they brought to the game. These two traits would come to define the Orchard in the years that followed.

Brian McAlinden told the press afterwards that there had been 'no heart, no fight' in Ballybofey, but it was damn evident in Tuam.

The four standout players were telling. Jarlath Burns, Kieran McGeeney, Paul McGrane and Diarmaid Marsden. The last two had found the net, with John Rafferty also getting in on the act.

Words in a dressing room can only bring you so far. Manifestation into on-field performances was the clearest indication that a special journey had begun.

'I barely touched my Christmas dinner. I trained like mad all over Christmas, and we actually came back after the Christmas break really, really fit,' says Burns.

'In one of our first training sessions in 1999, we went to Barnett's Park. When the training session was over, we were nearly back at the cars and Brian McAlinden said he wanted us to do one more thing. You've switched off at this stage as a player, your guard is down, so this is the last thing you want to hear.

'He said, "See that tree up there? I want you to run up there five times." This tree was up the biggest hill you'd see. About 400 metres to the top.

'It was a test of your resilience, he said. "Get up to the top, you can take a rest and walk back down. Do it five times."

'We went up and back down, wrecked; up the second time too. On the third one, he was at the top and he said, "I only want you to do three." We all turned around and said, "No, we're doing five," and we did. I would see that as another seminal moment.

'It's all about muscle memory. You start thinking I've done the work, so I owe this to myself.'

A loss, draw and win were followed by four straight wins on the resumption. Armagh found themselves top of the Division One Group A table.

That set up a quarter-final with lowly Sligo, in Longford in April 1999. Crossmaglen had won their second All-Ireland title weeks earlier, and their players were still mostly absent, although John McEntee did come off the bench late in the first half.

The game with the Yeats County reflected the horrendous weather conditions. Cathal O'Rourke put over four frees in the first period, and David Wilson was a rare ray of light, with two points from play, leaving Armagh on 0-6 at the interval. The fact that Armagh didn't score in the second half, yet still won, summed up the paucity of attacking quality on display.

A semi-final with Dublin awaited at Croke Park, and those two clashes left Jarlath Burns with plenty to ponder.

A chest infection developed into double pneumonia in January, requiring a week in hospital. Despite feeling 'weak as water', Burns raced back to county training as soon as he could. When the Dublin matches appeared on the horizon, his energy levels were completely sapped.

The drawn encounter was notable for a number of reasons. Firstly, it was played after the first semi-final, between Cork and Meath. In one of the lowest scoring games of modern times, the Rebels won 0-6 to 0-3.

The Armagh players caught glimpses of the game while preparing for their own encounter. Little did they know that the Meath team that managed only three points would play a big part in their own future.

Oisín McConville, who broke two knuckle bones in the All-Ireland Club final win over Ballina, pulled on the orange jersey for the first time that season and was the best player on the pitch against Dublin.

Armagh opted for some mental warfare by running down to warm up in front of the Hill. The Dubs joined them minutes later. The teams went hard at each other, in the second half in particular, to produce something akin to Championship intensity. It was McConville, filling the A.N. Other spot on the match programme, who kicked the levelling score.

However, Armagh's hate affair with Croke Park continued in the replay. Dublin dominated and Jarlath Burns felt he had reached the end of the road. No energy, no influence. It was time to retire.

Martin McQuillan, Martin Toye and Nial Smyth, three former Armagh captains with over 40 years' collective experience under their belts, had called it quits at the start of the 1998–99 season. Burns didn't think he would be missed given what he was reading in the papers either.

'It wasn't all sweetness in '99. It was tough. It was a very difficult pre-season, and there was a lot of recrimination. I felt sorry for those three servants,' Jarlath Burns says. 'People were writing in to papers. There were letters saying that I should retire, and disgraceful this and disgraceful that.'

There was a nagging voice at the back of his head, though: 'You've come this far; finish the season.'

Yet, just five weeks later, the end looked to be in sight, fittingly back in Ballybofey. At the venue where Armagh had locked themselves in and promised things would change, it seemed that nothing actually had.

Ronan Clarke had starred in the minor game, but Kevin McGlynn kicked a last-gasp winner for the hosts. And after seven minutes of the senior game, it looked like it would be double delight for Donegal.

'Taxi for Tierney,' Benny Tierney called out to anyone within earshot as John Duffy slotted the ball past him early on. Donegal 2-1 Armagh 0-0. Same old, same old. Words followed by a lack of action.

Only this time, Armagh didn't crumble. By half-time, the gap was back to just three points.

That recovery owed much to the introduction of Diarmaid Marsden after just 15 minutes. The Lurgan man had carried a groin injury into the Dublin replay and aggravated it badly. There was no way he should have been playing, but when the call went out, he put his body through hell and produced a stunning performance to keep the game, and the season, alive.

'Diarmaid Marsden wasn't fit and said he had only 20 minutes,' Brian Canavan recalls. 'I went into the dug-out after 15 minutes and said, "Diarmaid, you're going to have to go on now." There was no backdoor back then.'

As the team returned to the same dressing room where they had laid it all on the line after that recent National League defeat, a thought bulldozed its way into the mind of Jarlath Burns: 'This could be my last half-time speech for Armagh.'

'I said two things: "Lads, remember that day we went to the top of the hill to that fucking tree? Did we do that in vain? Was that a waste of time?

'The second question: "Am I walking out for the last half after 13 years with nothing, absolutely nothing?"'

What they walked out with was a replay. Four points down with as many minutes to go, Armagh rallied and twice appeared to have won it, only to be denied by scores from Brian Roper and then Michael Hegarty after Paddy McKeever had kicked what appeared to be the clincher.

It was the day when John McEntee announced himself to the Armagh fans. It was the day when Jarlath Burns vindicated his decision to stay on, as he picked up the Man of the Match award. It was a day when the Orchard County showed fight.

So often, Armagh's bottle had been questioned. They were viewed as a team that wilted in the big moments, like in the closing stages of Derry in 1998. To resurrect themselves from such a precarious position felt like a turning point.

Rather than wait until Tuesday's training, they met up on the Monday evening to chat about the game. A plan for the replay in Clones was already being formed.

That plan undoubtedly called for a quicker start, yet they still fell into the trap.

Thirty minutes in and Armagh were not only four points behind but a man down, as Oisín McConville was red carded for an alleged strike on Niall McCready. Donegal also lost a man, Martin Coll, who was sent to the line in unusual circumstances. As the second half began, referee

Mick Curley issued a second yellow card for a tackle he made at the end of the first half.

Once again for Armagh, it was left to the bench to rescue the situation, with Marsden coming forward to raise the tempo in the second half, while Cathal O'Rourke also had a huge influence. Between them they scored 2-1 to change the outcome of the game.

'I felt I let the team down last week, I just didn't perform at all,' O'Rourke said afterwards.

Lying in wait in the semi-final once again were Derry, the side that had defeated them in 1987, 1995, 1996 and 1998. In fact, Armagh's last championship win over the Oakleaf County had come in the 1977 Ulster final. Only one person in the dressing room, Brian McAlinden, had experience of beating Derry in the premier competition.

They had a bone to pick first. The county were adamant that McCready had made a meal of the early red card incident. They insisted that McConville hadn't struck, or made an attempt to strike, the player.

'Oisín was wrongly sent off,' Canavan said. 'McCready lay down right beside him.'

'I went up to Croke Park and they showed the video, and it was obvious he hadn't touched him.'

The attacker personally attended the meeting along with Canavan and County Board official Gene Duffy. After combing through the evidence, including video footage, the GAA's Games Administration Committee were satisfied that McConville was innocent. They noted that referee Mick Curley had not seen the incident and had acted on the word of one of his officials.

Donegal's Martin Coll was also exonerated, as his first yellow card was wiped out. Donegal briefly flirted with the idea of appealing the result to the Ulster Council, but the fact that Armagh had played with 14 men for so long meant that it was never a serious runner.

'I was sent off in the replay, and Ger Houlahan came into the changing room and said, "You were our only hope; we're fucked now," and I just thought, "Don't say that."' says McConville.

'I wanted another crack, and luckily enough I got that. That was in and around the time where the penny firmly dropped as a team.

'We lose that first game in Donegal and people go to their clubs and it's a long time until you gather up again and any momentum you had built goes.'

While Armagh didn't have the rub of the green with officials against Donegal, they could have few complaints as they finally laid the ghost of Derry to rest – and of course it had to be McConville that scored the crucial goal.

The other key moment came in the game's opening minute as Armagh's habitual slow start saw Derry awarded a penalty.

Gary Coleman stepped up to it, but was denied by an acrobatic Benny Tierney save. The Mullaghbawn man, this time in a yellow-and-blue Tetris special, stole four steps forward and flung himself high and to the right to tip the ball over the bar.

Derry were the sharper side, but errant shooting and McConville's first-half goal meant that they couldn't shake off their dogged opposition in an intensely physical confrontation.

With one minute to go, and Derry leading thanks to a fine score from Joe Cassidy, youngster Paddy McKeever picked up possession, toe-tapped past Gary Coleman and was absolutely cleaned by a bone-crunching – but fair – Henry Downey shoulder.

Cathal O'Rourke's trusty left foot levelled things up from the resulting free. Moments later, he set up the hitherto quiet Marsden to pop over the score that took Armagh to their first provincial final in nine years.

Jarlath Burns, who had gotten into the habit of meeting diehard supporters Ciaran Hughes and Claire Keenan after games as the Armagh fans invaded the pitch, celebrated wildly. After giving his jersey to Claire, supporters carried him bare-chested to the changing rooms.

At training the following Tuesday, Kieran McGeeney approached him.

'Were you carried off the pitch half-naked?' Geezer asked.

'I was,' Burns replied.

'What the fuck were you at?' Geezer responded with a shake of the head.

'Geezer, Mr Cool Head, ran into the dressing room right after the game,' said Burns. 'I was 13 years at this; I totally got caught up and had never experienced it before. My opinion was to celebrate it after the match and then get back to training the Tuesday night and bust a gut. Allow yourself the chance to celebrate it.'

Tyrone and Down met in the other semi-final, with the Red Hands expected to prevail. However, Ciaran McCabe, the Mourne County's 1994 super-sub, delivered a performance for the ages and Down won through.

Sweat broke out on Jarlath Burns's head every time McCabe sent a dagger through Tyrone hearts. He was spooked as he landed at Armagh's next training session after their final opponents had been confirmed.

He had a concern. No matter how out-of-form Down seemed, any sniff of confidence could turn them into world beaters in the blink of an eye – and he let his team know this.

'Before the final, I started talking in training. I said that we have a mental block against Down – they beat us in 1991, 1992; we've always struggled, and we need to do a bit of work on our mental resilience given that it's Down.

'The younger lads were looking at me weird and they said, "We've never been beaten by Down." And then it hit me that I'm the old one here, and these young lads have come through underage hammering Down. That reassured me. They had no hang-ups about Down, no inferiority complex.'

Brian McAlinden shared in that confidence, and his mind jolted back to the 1990 Armagh county final when, as player-manager, he had guided Sarsfields to their one and only county title against Armagh Harps.

'When our Sarsfields team left our pitch that Sunday morning to play, we didn't know what the actual score would be, but we were certain that there was no way we were coming home defeated,' said McAlinden.

'We had that mentality going to Clones that day against Down. It didn't matter how many All-Ireland titles Down had in the past; we just had in our minds total focus that we were going to win the Ulster Championship.

'Nothing was going to stop us. The guys put a lot of effort in and they had real pride in the jersey that hadn't been there for a while.'

That effort belonged not only to the players, with the management doing everything in their power to ensure that they were ready for the big occasion too – including enlisting the help of some of the GAA's most noted personalities.

'We had dinner with Ger Loughnane, who was over the Clare hurlers at the time, and that was just inspirational,' said McAlinden. 'His presence even in the hotel, he attracted a lot of attention. He's a great character; you could have sat there all day.

'We drove down the next day to Larry Tomkins's pub and met Larry. Just listening to those people was such a help.'

Loughnane stressed the need for winning sides to possess internal steel. This was music to the ears of the management.

'One thing Ger said to us, and it's something we put into practice, was that he refereed all in-house games himself,' says McAlinden. 'If some guy got hurt during the course of a game, the physio came on but he didn't stop the play, he just played on. There was a hardness about Clare at that time.

'He started the match and he stopped the match at the end of it, and that was it. That produced a steeliness, it made the players harder. The players played around, under, over injured players, and we tried to do that ourselves.

'In our in-house games, we let them play to just inside the law. We let them bend the rules of the game to breaking point and slightly beyond. There was a fierce rivalry there and a fierce will to win.

'I remember Kieran McGeeney and Justy McNulty fighting one night when they were both playing for Mullaghbawn, and I just let them finish it because there was no point in stopping it. We played on while they were buffing each other on the ground. That was the sort of intensity that was there in those in-house games.'

It wasn't just GAA legends that the pair sought counsel from. It may surprise a few to learn that former Rangers manager – Glasgow, not Crossmaglen – Dick Advocaat offered the two Brians a few hints and tips while he was in charge of the Ibrox club.

A Lurgan contact, John Byrne, had helped arrange for Armagh to travel to Celtic's training ground at Barrowfield. He was friendly with a golfing buddy of the Hoops' majority shareholder, Dermot Desmond.

The team were booked into The Crutherland House in East Kilbride, where Martin O'Neill was staying. The two Brians headed over a few days early to see if they could get a chat with the Derry man.

'Canavan had checked with Martin's brother, Gerry, to see where he was staying. Gerry would have been the Armagh manager when I played in '77 and he was obviously very familiar with the Gaelic scene,' said McAlinden.

'We booked in the Wednesday before we went. Martin O'Neill had to move out for a few days, because Rangers were there – they were playing in a European game.

'Dick Advocaat was the manager of Rangers, and we asked the general manageress would there be any chance of getting a chat. She said she would email him, and we got a response saying, "Yeah, no problem."

'He gave us an itinerary for what to do pre-match – meals and that sort of thing. It wouldn't have been much different from what we were doing.

'We had a chat with him. He wasn't totally familiar with Gaelic, but he would have been aware of Croke Park. It was nice to switch codes and see what others were doing.

'The following week, we met Martin O'Neill and myself and Brian had a bite of lunch with him.

'We had a couple of good sessions in Barrowfield. The Celtic senior team, Henrik Larsson and all, were coming off the field as we were coming on, and they couldn't believe that we were amateurs.'

Everything that happened on and off the pitch in the lead up to the 1999 Ulster final convinced Armagh that defeat was essentially impossible.

The Mourne County did manage to play a trump card in the warm-up. Captain James McCartan had been ruled out by manager Pete McGrath due to a disc issue in his back in the days beforehand. But, wearing the number 25, he took part in the pre-match kick-about before coming on for the last ten minutes. By then, the game was long gone.

Armagh had spent the weekend before the match in Sligo. One can only assume they resided in the spa, given how relaxed they appeared about the decider.

Oisín McConville and Diarmaid Marsden combined for a stunning 3-9.

'That's the day we also realised the genius of Messi and Ronaldo,' Jarlath Burns said of their performance. 'Diarmaid Marsden in that match, what that man did was sensational. Oisín was the man who scored, but the performance of Marsden was just incredible.'

Armagh players were often taken aback by Marsden's craving for work. Come back with your shield, or on it. Never go back into that dressing room without squeezing out every possible morsel of effort. He lived by those rules.

'Marsden's ability to understand that the first line of defence was the full-forward line was one of the biggest drivers for us winning,' Burns added.

'The two halves of the game are not the two chronological halves. Half one is what you do when you have the ball, and half two is what you do when your opponents have the ball.

'I remember Geezer saying to me that Diarmaid Marsden will never complain about the type of ball that goes into him. He was just one of those lads who could make something out of nothing. He had so many tricks up his sleeve. His ability to dispossess by tackling matched, and was nearly better than, his ability as a forward.'

Oisín McConville's 2-7 tally went down in folklore. It broke the 20-year record for the highest score in an Ulster final, previously held by Kieran Finlay for the stunning 1-9 he managed for Monaghan in the 1979 decider against Donegal.

Like Burns, McConville was keen to point to his partner in crime.

'A lot of what happened that day was just Diarmaid first of all reassuring me. I had marked Finbar Caulfield in a League match, and I thought he done quite well on me. He had bullied me in a way.

'I remember saying to Diarmaid that he may be marking me, and Diarmaid said, "Don't worry, he'll definitely be marking me." So I never thought any more about it.

'He did a huge amount of groundwork for me that day.

'I played well that day, but I had better games. The Ulster final in 2002 against Donegal was one of my better games, although it didn't stand out and didn't get the recognition – not that I was looking for it, but people maybe looked at it and saw it as an ordinary performance.

'The 1999 final was brilliant for me though. I knew Jap Finlay, and had met him coincidentally weeks before the final. I always knew he had the record and it was pretty much unbeatable. I hadn't a clue about the record when playing the game. I met him again after it and he congratulated me.'

Armagh led 2-5 to 0-6 at the break, but Marsden and McConville put their boot on Down's throat in the third quarter.

A train of Armagh scores was disrupted by the odd bit of drama in the second half.

When Andrew McCann failed to release the ball late on, Ross Carr took exception. When Brian McAlinden got involved, jostling broke out and when shoved in the face by the two-time Down All-Ireland winner, the Armagh joint-manager hit the deck.

Laid out on his back, James McCartan leaned down and hit him a slap on the cheek and told him to get up. McAlinden, a good friend of James McCartan Snr, sprang up with a devilish grin on his face and a hug for McCartan. Carr was yellow-carded.

The second issue sent shivers down those Armagh supporters who were of a pessimistic disposition. When Cathal O'Rourke released John McEntee for Armagh's penultimate point, hundreds of orange jerseys streamed onto the pitch.

Down net-minder Mickey McVeigh didn't wait for those fans to be cleared and pumped the ball forward as the Mourne County went in search of the miracle finish.

When the ball was booted towards the Armagh goal, not only did McCartan make an extraordinary catch under pressure from three Orchard defenders, but he had fans and stewards to find a way around too.

Some clad in orange still in the terraces feared the worst. Beaten down over the years by disappointment after disappointment, this fan incursion was simply an opportunity for match referee Paddy Russell to abandon the game. That early whistle would surely come, the players would be taken off the pitch and Down would undoubtedly win the refixture. The bill for Murphy's Law was proposed in the House of Armagh.

When Tony McEntee raced clear for the final score of the game, on the fans came again and those watching in the stands and on TV were treated to the unusual sight of players fisting the ball over stewards' heads to find a teammate.

The game finished though, the scoreboard reading 3-12 to 0-10 at the end. Considering Paul McGrane hit the crossbar and Oisín McConville butchered a glorious goal chance in the final seconds, Down got off lightly.

At the next training session, McAlinden filleted McConville for trying to chip Mickey McVeigh in the final moments instead of taking it around him and finishing to the net. But the Crossmaglen man had just broken the scoring record, and so was emboldened enough to firmly fight his corner.

'Certainly there was pride that day, but in a way myself and Brian would have been a bit disappointed that we didn't beat Down by more, because you don't get many opportunities to beat them,' McAlinden said about the argument.

'I know there was 11 points in it, but we weren't content with that to be honest. Oisín and myself had a bit of a barney about it. I wouldn't have been happy beating Down by 11 when we could have beaten them by 14.'

The winning margin mattered little to the thousands of Armagh fans who descended upon the Clones pitch when the full-time whistle sounded. A one-point win would have fulfilled their dreams just as much as the 11-point margin did.

Jarlath Burns could only shake his head in disbelief as the Anglo Celt was presented to him. He raised it in front of a sea of orange, his long journey finally rewarded with some silverware, those 13 years now justified.

Armagh had their first Ulster title in 17 years. One dream had been realised. Could another arrive in the coming weeks?

Chapter Four

The Hoodoo

A picture taken at the end of the 1999 All-Ireland semi-final between Armagh and Meath gave an insight into the mental fragility of Oisín McConville at that point.

Captured by Aoife Rice, on duty for Sportsfile at Croke Park, it shows McConville slumped to the ground, his head buried in the hallowed turf. Meath player Paddy Reynolds is bent over him, one hand on each of the Armagh man's sides, commiserating. McConville had had a nightmare day, and the Orchard County had bowed out of the race for Sam.

Nobody in the crowd was berating him. This, after all, was a man who had just lost his father, yet still came to play for his county in their biggest match in 17 years.

Patsy McConville wasn't dead though. Rumours had swept around the crowd that he had lost his battle with illness in the lead-up to the game, but the information was wide of the mark. Patsy passed away a few days later.

His father's sickness was just the latest thing troubling McConville at that time. The gambling problem that had taken hold was growing into a more serious addiction with every week that passed.

'It was tough, but I suppose emotionally I wasn't where I needed to be at that time. I was just supressing all that stuff. I was dimming it down, sitting on it, bottling it up – all of those things,' McConville said.

'It wasn't registering in the way it should have been. I don't even have the get-out clause to say I was shite against Meath because I was constantly thinking about my father. I wasn't. I was thinking about how I buried things. I was thinking about owing money, destroying things along the way. I was in a dark place and I thought that was as low as it could go, but it got darker.

'It got way darker than that, but emotionally, if I'm telling my story, I always talk about my father's death. It is an example of where I was emotionally and how I was stunted.

'It was steady downhill from there. There were no more peaks and troughs, it was all downhill. From '99 more or less on, it was all downhill in terms of gambling, the attitude and, at times in the process, my football suffered.'

Just a few weeks earlier, McConville was the King of Clones. White collar turned up, St Tiernach's Park was his manor as he trampled all over Down.

Having had his name plastered across the papers following his record-breaking 2-7 Ulster final haul, here he was hitting the headlines again in altogether different circumstances.

'I didn't play well, even though I had a good amount of touches. My head just wasn't right, but I definitely would have played it again.

'I felt a bit like I was grieving on a national stage, even though my father hadn't died at that stage; he didn't die until the Wednesday. I was grieving for my father and myself and the way things were in my life.'

McConville linked up late with the Armagh team ahead of that Meath game, arriving down to Dublin on the Saturday evening. Team captain Jarlath Burns could see the weight of the world on his teammate's shoulders, and the pair went for a walk to try to clear some of the fog.

'I don't have a toothbrush with me,' was the first thing McConville said to Burns.

'Some of Oisín's frees barely got off the ground that day, and can you blame him?' Burns says.

McConville wasn't the only player who maybe should have reconsidered togging out in orange that day. Just before the end of normal time, with the Royals all but assured a final spot with Cork, Alan O'Neill came on to replace Paul McGrane.

Through their gloomy mood, the Armagh fans afforded him a warm welcome. He had suffered what had looked like a serious neck injury in the Ulster semi-final win over Derry. It was surprising to see him back on the pitch already.

The roots of the injury actually stemmed back to a match with his club Culloville in 1996, when a collision left him with a bruised spinal cord. The Derry match saw the injury flare up once again.

'I ended up in the Mater Hospital for two weeks. The doctors did a lot of tests on me and the bruising was back again. The fact was that the cord was damaged and I was advised to reconsider playing football,' O'Neill said.

'The doctor took me up to a spinal unit where there were 13 people, and something like 12 were paralysed. He was more or less saying, this is the reality of this injury. That really hit home, as you can imagine.

'At that age, you're just desperate to play football, but with the passing of time it was definitely foolish. I remember there being some discussion with the neurosurgeons about what level of contact would be acceptable, which gave me some sense of hope, but inter-county football was a big no-no.

'Tierney used to jibe me that I was going around every doctor in the country until I got one that said I'd be okay to play! I never actually got that clearance, but it was a really exciting time to be playing with Armagh and you just wanted to be part of it.'

His doctor made it quite plain that O'Neill would be risking paralysis if he did not hang up the boots instantly. In a follow-up letter discussing a meeting held between the pair 17 days before the Meath match, his doctor reiterated the risks.

'As you know, you have a congenitally narrowed cervical canal at the C4–C6 Level [i.e. the mid part of the neck],' it began. The letter went on to state that contact sport would bring with it a 'significant risk' of cervical paralysis. It finished: 'I sincerely hope you will make the correct decision with regards to your own health.'

O'Neill did not. He risked possibly spending the rest of his life in a wheelchair just for that buzz of playing.

'It was stupid now, looking back, but I was just desperate to play. We were after winning the Ulster U21, and I knew the quality was there with the older players to win the All-Ireland. It's just a pity the way it worked out, but look, it could have been an awful lot worse.

'I did represent my county though. I didn't have the county career I wanted, but I have a couple of Ulster medals, played in two All-Ireland semi-finals and, more importantly, I got to know a deadly group of lads. There were players a lot better than me that didn't get to experience that, so I've lots to be thankful for.

'I also got a job I love and met a great wife, and I think that was helped by being part of Armagh at the time,' he adds with a laugh.

At the end of the following year, O'Neill started experiencing numbness in his arms and thumbs, and he went for further tests. His county career would soon come to an end, but after a leave of absence of a few years, he returned to the club scene and played for a few more seasons.

By the time O'Neill entered the fray against Meath, Armagh's season was in its dying embers.

A sea of orange had descended on Croke Park and, for a few magic minutes, the Royals had struggled against them to stem the tide. Brian McAlinden and Brian Canavan made a number of changes tactically for the game, but there was a personnel change that some in the panel felt had been a mistake when the dust settled on the season.

John Rafferty was regarded in football circles as a safe pair of hands. Hard-working and versatile, he was the sort of player who rarely hit a nine out of ten, but rarely dipped below seven. He could be brilliant, as demonstrated by his Player of the Tournament award when St Mary's won the 1989 Sigerson Cup, and managers loved his reliability. He was also an intelligent player, who knew the tactical strengths of the Armagh team. He had started in that unforgettable Ulster final win over Down, so changes were unexpected.

However, on the Thursday before the semi-final, he was hit with a bombshell. Dropped, with John Donaldson earning a starting call. Rafferty decided not to travel to the game, before ultimately being convinced by his family to do so.

'I disagreed with the decision at the time and I still do, because I was taken off the team and replaced by people who hadn't been there at the start of the National League, because Armagh wasn't important enough for them at that time,' he told the *Irish News* in 2021.

Donaldson had only joined the Armagh panel in May of 1999, following the conclusion of the National League campaign. He had played two League games for Crossmaglen, having transferred from Louth club Stabannon, and was drafted into the Orchard squad.

Donaldson had been part of the Orchard panel previously under Jim McCorry, while playing with Cullyhanna, but it was during his time with Louth that his reputation really started to grow. Viewed as an enforcer, Armagh fans were excited at the prospect of the steel he could add, with a growing clamour for his involvement. Management were no doubt influenced by those external calls, but the merits of their decision could be seen too.

In 1998, on the same afternoon that Derry were finishing strongly to kill off Armagh in Clones, Louth met Meath in the Leinster Championship semi-final at Croke Park and came within a point of Sean Boylan's side.

Donaldson wasn't 100 per cent fit heading into the game, but he had impressed at centre half-back with support from captain Gareth O'Neill at full-back, the future Crossmaglen manager and father to Orchard stars Rían and Oisín.

Where he was listed was also an indication of the tactics Armagh would adopt on the day. Donaldson, regarded as a defender, was named at midfield, while Jarlath Burns was stationed in a deeper role than usual. Diarmaid Marsden was positioned further from goal too. The plan was clear – flood the middle third and hit fast on the break.

In the Monday papers, those tactics in the 0-15 to 2-5 defeat were pulled apart, but for 24 minutes they had looked inspired. At that stage, Mardsen and Kieran Hughes had broken through for goals and the Ulster champions were leading 2-1 to 0-4.

Armagh would come unstuck in two major ways. Over the course of the game, their Achilles' heel – poor shooting when the pressure was on – reared its head again. More obvious, though probably less crucial given that Armagh were already struggling by that stage, was Ger Reid's dismissal in the 54th minute for a block on Graham Geraghty. When the Lurgan man was shown his second yellow card, Armagh were still ahead by a point, but the confidence was visibly seeping out of them.

Speaking now, Reid said Paddy Russell's decision to give him a second yellow was inevitable after a catalogue of errors. However, the first booking is the one that still hurts.

'I honestly don't know why I got the first yellow card,' says Reid. 'I think Geraghty was yapping to the linesman. There were no thumps or anything, just the usual pulling and slapping from both of us. Every time I niggled him, he went to the umpire, so I got booked and that was in the first half.

'If you get a booking you can look at it and see a pull down or a trip and you deserve it, but Paddy Russell could never tell me why I got that first booking.

'For the second one, a high ball came in and I was shoved, I've seen the video. I thought I would have been given a free but I wasn't. The ball dropped in front of me and I should have got it there. I tried to pick it up twice and fumbled it. The second time, I fumbled it into Geraghty's hands and I thought he was in on goal, so I dived in front of him and blocked him with my body.

'It was terrible what I did there, it was crazy. You'd give off to a child for doing it in an underage game, so you have to hold your hands up.'

On the day that Meath beat Armagh, Robbie Williams was headlining at Slane Castle. Geraghty, preoccupied with the small matter of an All-Ireland semi-final, didn't make it, but he was there three years later as The Red Hot Chilli Peppers topped the bill.

As he sipped a pint in the early afternoon sun, he was approached by an Armagh fan and berated for getting Reid sent off.

A few weeks earlier, Geraghty had left the top table of his best friend's wedding, hopped in a helicopter and flown to Navan for Meath's Qualifier with Louth. Still dressed in his best man attire, he raced to get changed and then scored the clinching goal to settle a bona fide classic.

So, finally getting the chance to relax after a hectic summer, Geraghty placated the young Armagh fan, telling him he felt bad that such a well-respected player would get sidelined in a big game. Inside, he must have been thinking, 'These Armagh lads have trouble letting things go.'

It summed up the Orchard County's season. They had ended their long wait for a provincial title, but the year had still finished in frustration. Was that their one shot at All-Ireland glory? Could the Orchard get back to the All-Ireland series?

They would have to attempt it without a bucket-load of experience, as previous captain Jarlath Burns and John Rafferty now decided enough was enough. Their efforts had been rewarded with an Ulster medal at least.

Kieran McGeeney was the obvious man to succeed Burns as skipper of the team, but the National League programme did not go smoothly.

The first six games brought zero victories, and the relegation trapdoor had already opened by the time they visited Dungannon for a meeting with

Tyrone in round seven. Safety was out of reach, but an away win, thanks in the most part to Mark McNeill's brilliant goal-line clearance from Peter Canavan, at least provided a morale boost ahead of the Ulster meeting between the rivals two months later.

Mentally, Armagh should have been in a different place. Their Ulster success in 1999 allowed them to cast off so many negative tags associated with the side, but they started the 2000 provincial campaign at a pedestrian pace.

Yes, Tyrone were dismissed by four points in the quarter-final, and victory over the Red Hands is never to be taken for granted, but Tyrone were still a year or two away from spending the profits of their fantastic underage success. It was a welcome scalp, but not a particularly notable one.

The semi-final wasn't much better, as they defeated Fermanagh 0-13 to 0-12. There was no shortage of perspiration, but inspiration was another question.

There were fleeting moments of positivity though. Barry 'Bumpy' O'Hagan, who had only been drafted into the Orchard panel the week before, came on when Diarmaid Marsden went off injured after 15 minutes. He was probably their best player on the day.

Another contender was corner-forward Stevie McDonnell, settling in nicely after breaking into the starting side. That he was positioned in attack was a relief to the player.

'I spent the whole of 1999 as number 30 or 31 on the panel,' McDonnell says. 'Myself and Aidan O'Rourke were the two players competing for the number 30 jersey. If you got 30, you were named in the programme for the Championship games; 31 wouldn't be.

'For that entire year, I was playing corner-back in training, the whole year.

Most of those training sessions, I was marking John Rafferty, a natural corner-back who was playing wing half-forward or corner-forward.

'It's ironic how things can turn, but I always look at that year as being crucial. It taught me to work hard. It thought me to value your natural position. It also taught me how to tackle and defend to an extent. I wasn't the best tackler or defender, but it helped.

'It taught me to make sure I took the opportunity when it presented itself.

'I remember numerous training sessions where the chance came to drive up the field, support the play and kick a couple of scores – to maybe show the two Brians that I was capable of doing that.'

Armagh's first score against Fermanagh saw McDonnell set Cathal O'Rourke up for a point, and the Killeavy man was happy to repay some of the debt that he owed to his club rival, now a county ally.

'One thing that stands out for me is the work Cathal O'Rourke did with me night after night when I first broke into the team. Cathal spent endless hours on endless nights kicking ball after ball in, and I was taking it first time and kicking it over my shoulder. That became a trademark score of mine down through the years.

'I hadn't anyone marking me. From time to time, Enda McNulty might stay on and shadow me, but he didn't get physical in those encounters. It was extra work.

'It was always a great pass from Cathal, but if I spilled a ball we didn't continue with it. I had to learn to trap that ball first time, learn to take good ball and dirty ball and get a shot off as quickly as I possibly could.'

Those direct balls were enough to finally fend off Fermanagh, and Armagh were back in the Ulster final. Derry – who they had edged in the semi-final the previous year – lay in wait in Clones, intent on revenge.

The Oakleaf County hadn't lost a competitive game since that 1999 defeat. Despite a massive scare from a rejuvenated Antrim in the 2000 semi-final, the National League champions were hotly tipped to be crowned kings of Ulster.

Armagh had been missing a spark on their way to the final, but things were ignited by a fist fight in the corridor as the two sides made their way to the dressing rooms.

Footballers are generally a superstitious bunch, and one dressing room under the stand at St Tiernach's Park was considered luckier than the other. Following a training session at the Monaghan venue the week before, Armagh joint manager Brian McAlinden had somehow ensured that their name was on the door of the lucky one.

Opposite number Eamonn Coleman wasn't happy when he found out, and a stand-off developed. Armagh officials pleaded with their team to go across the hall, but take that backward step then and the Orchard players may as well have raised the white flag and saved everyone the bother.

Negotiations broke down. Through a rain of punches, Armagh forced their way in and closed the door behind them.

'There was a punch up, but spectators didn't see it,' McAlinden said of the incident. 'County officials were looking us to go across the way, to go into the other dressing room, but we said no, we said we'd get onto the bus before we'd change.

'Eamonn was a wee bit superstitious like myself and knew that the dressing room on the left-hand side is classed as the winners' dressing room. Most people involved would have seen that; certainly Eamonn would have. I knew it was the one he wanted.

'He was in an agitated state, and I was trying to rub him up, to get him thinking of the wrong things, and it probably did work. There was no way we weren't going to take the dressing room. I let the heavyweights do the punching though.'

McDonnell properly announced himself onto the national stage that day, with the game's opening goal. His first championship strike – and Armagh's first goal of that year's Ulster campaign – was a thing of beauty.

Barry O'Hagan did well to field cleanly, and his clever over-the-shoulder fist pass sent McDonnell on through in the 14th minute. McDonnell took two steps, looked up and finished expertly to the top corner, beyond a despairing Eoin McCloskey.

The man nicknamed 'Stevie from Killeavy' would plunder a ridiculous 53 goals in 161 games in county colours.

Unlike the knife-edge semi-final of 1999, underdogs Armagh were clearly the better side. When they moved into a 1-11 to 0-9 lead in the third quarter, another comfortable Ulster final win looked on the cards.

However, while they had put the foot on the neck of Down 12 months earlier, now they allowed Derry to breathe again, tagging on just one more point. That was the winner though, coming via an Oisín McConville free four minutes from time.

Derry were presented with one last chance to draw level, but Anthony Tohill's effort from way out the field drifted right and wide, sparking wild celebrations from the Armagh fans, players and management.

Security had been beefed up at Clones and the traditional orange pitch invasion didn't materialise. The Anglo Celt was presented on the pitch rather than on the steps of the Gerry Arthurs stand, and the players embarked on a lap of honour. The McEntee twins followed Jarlath Burns's example of a year previous by discarding their jerseys.

'That 2000 team was the best Armagh ever had,' says Brian Canavan.

That claim may appear outlandish, given what unfolded two years later, but there could be more than an element of truth to it.

When it came to it, Kerry needed 170 minutes in all – extra time was 15 minutes each way then – to finally get past Armagh in the All-Ireland semi-final, before going on to claim their 32nd Sam Maguire success at the expense of Galway.

Armagh v Kerry presented two stone-cold classics at Croke Park. Some 31 counties cheered an Orchard outfit in their pursuit of their most famous win. Magic from Maurice Fitzgerald and one dropped shot into the goal-keeper's hands would define the series.

Páidí Ó Sé's side were sparkling up to that point. Dara Ó Cinnéide grabbed a brace of penalty goals as they racked up a strong 2-15 tally in the Munster semi-final against perennial rivals Cork. After that, Clare were never going to bother them in the provincial final. The Banner were hit for 3-15.

The crescendo of noise that rose towards the end of 'Amhrán na bhFiann' was spine-tingling. Benny Tierney, kitted out in the same bright luminous jersey that he had worn against Derry, chomped wildly on chewing gum, Ger Reid took a series of deep breaths on what was his 30th birthday. The Armagh fans in the stadium erupted in a call to arms.

Twelve months earlier, Armagh had allowed a golden opportunity to slip through their fingers. Now they were back and ready to face Gaelic football's aristocrats.

Kerry provided a swift reminder of their class just 15 seconds into the contest. Darragh Ó Sé pushed aside John McEntee to claim referee John Bannon's throw in, before playing it forward to Mike Frank Russell, who had given Enda McNulty the slip. The man who had caused so many of the

Armagh squad major headaches in the 1994 All-Ireland Minor semi-final cut in and split the posts with ease.

From Benny Tierney's kick-out, Kerry broke forward again and with Ger Reid affording Dara Ó Cinnéide too much space, the Kingdom forward blasted towards goal, only to see his effort pushed to safety by the Armagh net-minder.

Kieran McGeeney tried to relieve the pressure from the rebound but when his kick-pass was blocked down, Kerry broke and were awarded a penalty when Andy McCann felled Johnny Crowley as he bore down on goal. When Ó Cinnéide sent Tierney the wrong way, the goalkeeper's expletive was picked up with amazing clarity by the RTÉ microphones and relayed to the watching public. 'Taxi for Tierney' was too jovial a response in the circumstances, even for Tierney.

John McEntee was next to be blocked down, which led to Crowley making it 1-2 to 0-0 just four minutes in.

The Kerry pressure was immense. Enda McNulty, not noted for his kick-passing, had no option but to boot the ball down the field. Kerry picked up possession, came forward at pace and Ó Cinnéide sliced over a gorgeous effort.

Six points down in as many minutes. The Ulster champions were knee deep in quicksand.

Like Ger Reid, it was Brian Canavan's birthday too, but he wasn't in a party mood as he cut a disconsolate figure on the sideline.

It was youth rather than experience that settled everyone down, as Paddy McKeever's cultured left foot raised their first white flag of the day after selling Tomás Ó Sé a beautiful dummy. That acted as the smelling salts, as Armagh came to after their initial pummelling. It was soon game on.

Cathal O'Rourke's long pass towards McKeever was broken away well, but Stevie McDonnell was able to flick the loose ball back to the Bally-hegan man. Two versus one, he fisted across goal to Barry O'Hagan, who drove low past Declan O'Keefe for his first championship goal.

O'Rourke, who had a monster of a first half despite shipping some big hits, pinged over two frees off the deck with his trusty left foot to square matters up. The first time he was chopped down, the television cameras panned to the crowd and by pure chance focussed on his parents – who were looking more than worried for their kin – and his younger brother Micheál, who would eventually become the fourth O'Rourke brother to represent his county.

Mike Frank Russell ended Kerry's 20-minute wait for a score and the Kingdom turned on the afterburners to race four points clear as the interval loomed, only for Oisín McConville to slice over when he should have rattled the net, leaving it 1-7 to 1-5 at the break.

Seconds after the restart, the gap was back to one, as Tony McEntee stroked over in the twins' typically languid style. McConville then levelled it up from a free. Kerry's response was to bring in Maurice Fitzgerald, and they moved a point ahead.

Seconds later, a wall of noise to make the hairs on the back of your neck stand to attention reverberated around the ground. Kerry had called on Fitzgerald, but Armagh had their own ace in the hole in Diarmaid Marsden.

The introduction of those two players cranked up the decibel levels, but while still exciting, the standard of football over the next 20 minutes plummeted. The exception was the two men with number three on their backs.

For Kerry, Seamus Moynihan was claiming everything that came his way. He sent Kieran Hughes flying with a hefty shoulder charge at one stage as the Pearse Óg man bore down on goal.

In the book Kerry: Game of My Life by David Byrne, Moynihan identified this match as the most significant of his career. He was only parachuted into full-back after Barry O'Shea tore his cruciate in a League game against Roscommon five months earlier, but would finish the season as Footballer of the Year.

At the other end was birthday boy Ger Reid, driven by the desire to make up for his red card disappointment of the previous year. He was constantly getting out in front of the Kerry forwards to intercept.

Armagh owned possession, but wayward shooting forced the umpires to stretch their arms wide time and time again. The ghosts of Meath 1999 were floating around the minds, doubts bubbling below the surface.

Those fears were only ratcheted up when Marsden found himself through on goal, but instead of the net bulging, he drove the ball straight at the legs of Declan O'Keeffe.

Neither side could get away as the second half continued. Páidí Ó Sé, clad in that famed yellow polo top with 'Bainisteoir' blazoned across it, looked nervous as he paced the sideline, a youthful selector by the name of Jack O'Connor never too far away from him. Nor was Brian McAlinden. Anytime Po, as Páidí was known to friends and family, went for a walk along the touchline, the Armagh joint-manager followed him. No chance a coincidence.

That Kingdom apprehension disappeared in the blink of an eye, however, as the game entered its final quarter. Noel Kennelly put them back in front after referee John Bannon ignored a clear penalty for Johnny Crowley in the build-up, following a foul by Kieran McGeeney.

From the resulting kick-out, Kerry quickly won possession and worked it forward to Crowley out on the wing. He slipped a fist pass to Maurice Fitzgerald, coming in from the Cusack sideline. The silky St Mary's man went on a purposeful run past Justin McNulty, Kieran McGeeney and Kieran Hughes and beautifully picked his spot. 2-10 to 1-9.

The parallels with the Meath semi-final were all too obvious, but they wouldn't hold. Armagh weren't ready to wilt yet.

Crowley dummied John McEntee and was left with a seemingly simple point, only for the Crossmaglen man to somehow get a hand in. Desire. A sloppy pass was played forward to Cathal O'Rourke, but he somehow won a 40/60 ball in front of Tomás Ó Sé to earn a free. Determination. Next, McGeeney took a Tierney kick-out over three Kerry players closing in. Doggedness.

O'Rourke landed a free to bring Armagh back within a goal with eight minutes left. And then it came – pure pandemonium.

Armagh had created 32 scoring chances to Kerry's 21, but still trailed by three points when Andy McCann snaffled a loose ball, put the head down and raced towards the Canal End. He passed to substitute Alan O'Neill, with the ball moving on to Oisín McConville and then Diarmaid Marsden.

Aware that, with just a minute left, going for broke was now a necessity, McCann continued his run. He took the ball back from Marsden, stepped inside a desperate Kerry tackle and fired low past Declan O'Keeffe.

The foundations of Croke Park shook. They nearly fractured altogether when Kieran McGeeney came off the shoulder of McConville, took the ball and clipped over with his left moments later.

On the bench, Stevie McDonnell, Paddy McKeever and Cathal Short stood arm in arm. McKeever's smile was one of a man who felt that John

Bannon's full-time whistle was coming. John Donaldson stood with one hand on Aidan O'Rourke's shoulder.

Tierney launched a free long and surely the whistle would follow, but it didn't. No matter, Alan O'Neill rose and took the ball cleanly. John McEntee ate up another few seconds and fed the ball out right to Barry O'Hagan near the touchline.

O'Hagan looked up and scanned his options. He could race up the sideline and take the ball to the corner or he could go for glory. The Clan na nGael man opted for the latter. While he had the accuracy, he didn't have the distance and the ball dropped into Declan O'Keeffe's hands.

John Bannon didn't bail him out. The ball was worked up the field and Dara Ó Cinnéide was tackled. Free in. Soft. Routine for someone like Maurice Fitzgerald, and the teams were level for a sixth time. Kerry somehow survived. Armagh had somehow failed to land the knockout blow.

'I played one of my better games for Armagh that day. I was at 11 and was being marked by Eamonn Fitzmaurice and I scored 1-2 from play,' says O'Hagan. 'We all played reasonably well, but the criticism at the end was probably warranted. Looking back now, it was definitely warranted. When the ball left my boot, I thought it was going over the bar. I couldn't believe when it dropped short.

'It wasn't nice at the time, hearing that you would have been in an All-Ireland final if the ball had been put dead, but I should have been experienced enough to carry it in and win a free, or at least put it dead.

'They went up the field and won a free that Maurice Fitzgerald put over to draw. It didn't really affect me though. We didn't pay much attention to papers, and I think I scored the first point from play in the replay.'

The warm-up act in that replay saw an 18-year-old Cora Staunton treating the crowd to an exhibition as she hit 3-6 in the ladies' semi-final. That she did it against Tyrone didn't hurt either, in the view of the Armagh fans who had made it to the ground early.

Afterwards, in the pubs around Jones' Road, Armagh and Kerry supporters would watch together as Mick McCarthy's Republic of Ireland side left Amsterdam with a 2-2 draw after a brilliant World Cup Qualifier performance against the Netherlands.

In between those two occasions, over 50,000 fans savoured the best entertainment of that sporting day.

As the Orchard squad made their way onto the pitch, chests puffed out, Stevie McDonnell's body language was less positive, with the white tracksuit top of a substitute covering his orange jersey. McDonnell had burst onto the scene in Ulster, but, bar getting a crucial hand in in the lead-up to Armagh's first goal, Michael McCarthy had completely blotted him out in the drawn Kerry game.

He wasn't the only forward to have had a bad day at the office. After a bright start, Paddy McKeever's influence waned, while Oisín McConville's ten shots at goal had brought just three points. But it was McDonnell who made way to get Diarmaid Marsden into the starting team, and it's something that still eats at him.

'The biggest issue I would have with the two Brians – and listen, I don't hold a grudge against them – was dropping me for the Kerry semi-final replay,' he says. 'I went through the Ulster campaign that year and was very good; I was on the Irish News Ulster All-Star team.

'I played my first big match in Croke Park against Kerry and knew I was going to get taken off from an early stage. I wasn't at the races. I played the occasion rather than the match. I got too involved with the Croke Park scenario. Looking around me. I forgot that I was there to play a game of football.

'Mike McCarthy took me to the cleaners and I was pulled ashore with maybe 20 minutes to go, and deservedly so. But we drew that game and I felt that I had learnt my lesson.

'Diarmaid Marsden was coming back into the team after an injury and I knew I was going to be under pressure to keep my place.

'I got dropped. There were a couple of forwards who didn't have as good a season as I did, but the first opportunity the two Brians got to drop me, they dropped me. I was annoyed with that; it was hard to take as a young fella.

'I came on in the replay and scored two points. I came on and redeemed myself somewhat against a very good Kerry team. Unfortunately we lost the game; we had a great chance to win it, but we went on and lost.'

By the time McDonnell came on in the 65th minute, the game was on a knife-edge, the sides level after another rip-roaring hour-and-a-bit's football.

In what was now becoming a tradition, Armagh had started slowly, with Aodán Mac Gearailt putting the Kingdom ahead after 29 seconds.

Another marker had to be laid down in that opening minute, and Tomás Ó Sé did so by clattering into Cathal O'Rourke. He did it again in the fifth minute, and this time it was spotted by an umpire, with referee Brian White brandishing a yellow card.

In their post-match debrief after the drawn game, the Kerry players felt that the Dromintee man had been allowed to bully them about the pitch, particularly by blocking Darragh Ó Sé on kick-outs. They weren't going to let it happen again.

That focus nearly cost them though. In the 30th minute, Ó Sé fouled O'Rourke again along the sideline. This indiscretion was clumsy rather than vicious, but Brian White took his book out as he walked towards the player. Seeming to realise that he was already on a yellow, White opted for stern words instead.

Jarlath Burns describes the role that O'Rourke played for the team on kick-outs over the years.

'What Cathal O'Rourke would do for me around the middle was unbelievable,' he says. 'I'd go up and catch the ball and you'd hear this "ughh-hhhh", and it was Cathal coming in behind me and firing boys out of the road who he knew were going to come up and compete against me. He'd bust them and then they'd bust him. It's only when you'd watch the game back on TV that you'd see that he shipped a thump.

'In many games, I got Man of the Match for my catching, but it was Cathal doing all the work behind the scenes. A workhorse. Incredible.'

And Kerry were determined to curb O'Rourke's influence the second time around.

'The first ball that dropped, away he went – I was thinking, God he's doing it – so for the second ball I tore into him before it dropped out around the middle of the field, and he ended up on the ground. And that put a stop to it,' Tomás Ó Sé said in his autobiography The White Heat.

Winners walk the line and Kerry, for all the romance attached to them, were no different. It was a lesson Armagh would learn from for the 2002 final.

Back in the replay, Armagh won the next ball. A nice flowing move was finished off by the one man the two Brians would have picked to open their account – Barry O'Hagan.

Armagh captain Jarlath Burns becomes the first man from the Orchard County to lift the Anglo Celt Cup since 1982.

Above: Joe Kernan and the Crossmaglen players warm up for a training session in May 1998, with the British Armagh barracks pictured in the background.

Below: A dejected Oisín McConville, who would lose his father Patsy three days later, is consoled by Meath's Paddy Reynolds after their All-Ireland clash at Croke Park in August 1999.

Armagh's Cathal O'Rourke receives some close attention from Kerry's Tom O'Sullivan in the 2000 All-Ireland semi-final.

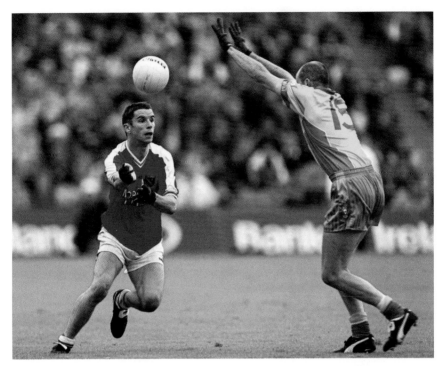

Above: Paul McGrane fists the ball past Paul McGonigle in the 2002 Ulster final between Armagh and Donegal.

Below: Referee Seamus McCormack receives a Garda escort from the field, having failed to award Sligo a late penalty in their 2002 All-Ireland quarter-final replay loss to Armagh in Navan.

Paddy McKeever bundles home Armagh's goal in their 1-14 to 1-13 All-Ireland semi-final win over Dublin in 2002.

Above: Armagh manager Joe Kernan holds court at the team's media night at the Athletic Grounds ahead of the 2002 All-Ireland final with Kerry.

Below: The Armagh team prior to the 2002 All-Ireland final against Kerry at Croke Park.

Above: Armagh's Oisín McConville celebrates scoring the only goal of the game in the 2002 All-Ireland final.

Below: Oisín McConville becomes the third Armagh player to miss a penalty in the All-Ireland final, as Kerry goalkeeper Declan O'Keefe saves his effort in the 2002 decider.

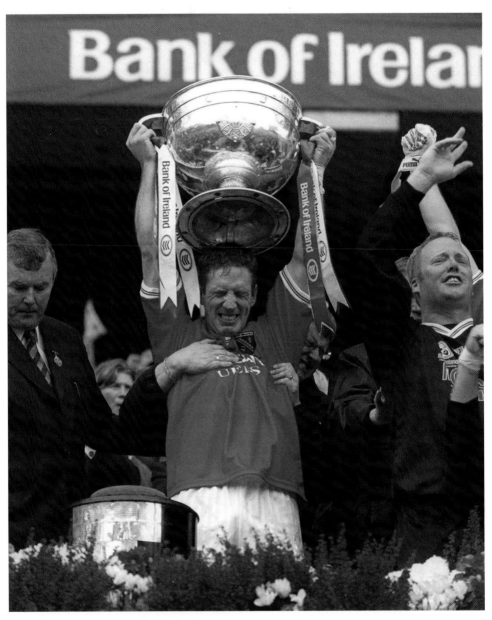

Kieran McGeeney becomes the first-ever Armagh player to lift the Sam Maguire Cup on All-Ireland final day.

The future Donegal U15 and Armagh U20 manager had butchered the chance to win the game the first day, and the ball sailing between the Hill 16 posts would have made him feel a lot better about himself. Not quite atonement, but some sort of restitution.

It took Armagh 69 minutes to lead in the drawn encounter, but just 15 in the replay as a fantastic point from Diarmaid Marsden left them 0-4 to 0-3 ahead. Four shots at goal, four points.

Their famed inaccuracy was replaced with ruthlessness as they led 1-7 to 0-6 at the turn. Eight scores from 10 shots was dreamland stuff for the Ulster champions.

The goal had come moments before half-time. With Moynihan lording it at one end, his opposite full-back, Ger Reid, played a massive role in the first green flag of the day.

Dara Ó Cinnéide's effort at a point was a tired one and the ball fell well short. Benny Tierney came out to claim, but completely misjudged it and spilled it into the air, where Aodán Mac Gearailt looked set to slap it into the net.

Reid somehow got a hand in to deflect the ball to John McEntee, who carried it out of defence. He played it to his younger brother – by only 30 minutes – Tony, who moved the ball on to Cathal O'Rourke. The half-forward put the head down and ate up 30 metres of ground before playing a delicate ball into Diarmaid Marsden. It wasn't the cleanest pass and the Clan na nGael man showed good strength to win the ball, before going around two defenders and offloading to the incoming Oisín McConville.

The Crossmaglen man's shot was perfect. So perfect that it bounced off the back of the goal stanchion and back into play. Many in Croke Park thought the ball had hit the post, leading to a strangely delayed reaction from the Orchard County fans. But it had hit the net alright, leaving Armagh with a commanding lead.

The opening minutes of the second half did little to deflect from the notion that Armagh had Kerry's number. The scoreboard didn't change and the Munster kingpins looked short on ideas and short on confidence.

They had that Maurice Fitzgerald-shaped rabbit still in their hat though, and it wasn't long before he was thrown in.

'There's a crisis in Kerry, Maurice Fitzgerald is coming in,' commentator Ger Canning told those watching on RTÉ.

And the crisis deepened a minute later, when John McEntee slotted over an excellent point in that lackadaisical, almost-couldn't-be-arsed style of his. The nervous energy of the Armagh crowd was transforming into belief.

On the pitch, however, Kerry now started to chip away at that confidence. Liam Hassett pointed, then Mike Frank Russell did likewise. A Maurice Fitzgerald '45' dropped short and was nearly scrambled to the net.

Armagh, just as they had done against Meath in 1999 and in Ulster in 2000, seemed to be dropping closer and closer to their own goal, inviting pressure on.

Fitzgerald split the posts with an outstanding free from near the Hogan sideline, given after a harsh over-carrying call on Kieran Hughes, and Éamonn Fitzmaurice came forward to leave just a point between the sides with 12 minutes remaining.

An exquisite Oisín McConville effort proved a brief moment of resistance as Mike Frank Russell took hold of Fitzgerald's perfectly weighted left-to-right delivery, swivelled and fired low to the net. Having been second-best for the majority of the contest, Kerry now led 1-10 to 1-9. McConville equalised from a free before Stevie McDonnell made his way on.

Dara Ó Cinnéide hit a fine score for Kerry before another McConville score levelled it as the game drifted into additional time. After four second-half substitutions and a few visits from both physios, four minutes had been added on to the 70 minutes – enough to see John McEntee's attempt at a winner land in Declan O'Keeffe's hand.

It took just five minutes of extra time for Kerry to all but kill off the game. After tagging on the opening two points, the ball was worked through to Mike Frank Russell. For the second time that Saturday afternoon, he coolly finished low to the corner. The scoreboard on the old Nally Stand read Ard Mhacha 1-11 Ciarraí 2-13.

Armagh were trying everything to get back into the game.

In 1984, Ger Houlahan had lined out alongside his current managers Brian McAlinden and Brian Canavan in the Ulster Championship in what became known as the 'Frank McGuigan final'. The Tyrone man scored 11 points in all: five with his left, five with his right and one fisted over the bar to secure the Anglo Celt for the Red Hands.

Sixteen years later, Houli, who had become a cult hero during the '90s for Armagh fans as he bagged goal after goal, was comfortable enough with his position as a fringe player on the squad that he gave an interview to RTÉ at half-time in extra-time. The rest of the Orchard players were huddled up for their team talk. Three minutes later he was on the pitch.

Armagh would outscore their opponents four points to two from Kerry's second goal, but it wasn't enough. Three points would separate the sides after 170 minutes. Of all the nearly moments they had experienced, this one perhaps carried the greatest weight of all.

They had a shot at saving the situation too. In the eighth minute of the second period, and with neither side registering a shot at goal since the extra-time break, Oisín McConville timed his run perfectly. He was clean through on the Canal End goal. It looked a certain three-pointer, but his effort was too central and Declan O'Keeffe denied him. Kerry went down and tagged on two scores in the following minute to end the game as a contest.

Having slumped to the ground in 1999 after playing in the most difficult of circumstances, McConville's full-time response in 2000 was to join in with the very sporting scenes between the two counties. The players swapped jerseys, shook hands and even enjoyed a few laughs heading off the pitch.

Armagh, just like in 1999, had lost. They had gotten closer this time, but their All-Ireland dream looked further away than ever.

Chapter Five

Tribal Warfare

T he engine kicked into gear and the Armagh team coach slowly pulled away from Croke Park in almost complete silence. As dejection filled the air, anger bubbled below the surface. In the coming weeks, that anger would give way to change, a change that would have a monumental impact on the Orchard County.

It was 7 July 2001. The quiet journey home was in complete contrast to just a few hours earlier, when chaos had reigned.

The introduction of the Qualifier system that season had given everyone a second chance. After falling on the home stretch against Tyrone to relinquish their Ulster title in May, Armagh made the most of the opportunity with backdoor wins over Down and Monaghan.

Galway lay in wait in round three. Given that the Tribesmen had lost the 2000 All-Ireland final to Kerry after a replay, the size of the task at hand was obvious. Everything would have to go smoothly if this Armagh team was to claim its first real statement win at Croke Park. Very little did.

Visits to the iconic stadium, then under redevelopment, were still rare in those days for the Ulster side, but Armagh had been up and down enough times to get into a routine. It couldn't be called a winning routine – the county hadn't won a Championship match at the venue since the 1977 All-Ireland semi-final replay against Roscommon – but each trip followed a similar pattern.

The plan was simple enough. Brian Canavan and Brian McAlinden would bring their panel to the Na Fianna clubrooms for a loosening-up session, then An Garda Síochána motorcycles would arrive to escort them for the 2.2-kilometre journey to Jones' Road.

Kieran McGeeney was playing with the Dublin club at the time and, given its proximity to HQ, it was a logical choice for a venue. The departure time had been carefully decided – they wouldn't leave for Croke Park too early, for fear of the side being overwhelmed by the surroundings, as Steven McDonnell had been in the drawn 2000 All-Ireland semi-final with Kerry, but there would still be a bit of wiggle room.

The team generally liked to arrive about an hour before throw-in. Players would have a short window to do what they wanted – they could stretch, go for a walk or take in some of the first game if there was one on. This opportunity wasn't there that day, as they were on the undercard, with the meeting of Mick O'Dwyer's Kildare and Sligo topping the bill. Even that decision would impact on Armagh on a day when everything came unstuck.

With the game due to start at 2.15pm, the Orchard panel boarded the team bus just before 1pm and waited for the escort to arrive. And then waited some more.

Crossmaglen sharp-shooter Oisín McConville was in his usual spot on the team coach, in a foursome with Stevie McDonnell, Kevin McElvanna and Benny Tierney with two seats facing two.

Minutes passed and still no movement. Tierney, the joker of the group, tried to ease the tension, but his attempts were met with polite smiles rather than the usual laughter.

'When Tierney went quiet we knew we were in trouble,' says McConville.

Time was suddenly flying by, while frantic mobile phone calls were made by officials at the front of the bus.

With no solution in sight, the decision was made to proceed without accompaniment. Armagh were behind schedule, but not drastically so. The bus pulled out of the Na Fianna grounds, turned onto Mobhi Road and then reality hit home as it came to a complete stop. Bumper-to-bumper traffic lay in their path.

'Literally we just weren't moving,' says McConville. 'Panic was setting in. If you see the top of the bus panicking you know you're in fucking trouble.

'We were trying to make light of it; Benny was cracking a few jokes. We were having a bit of fun, but obviously it gets very serious very quickly.

'It's a journey that's meant to take 20 minutes and then you look out the window and see officials trying to stop cars and you say to yourself, "Ah, for fuck's sake, is this really happening?"'

Aidan O'Rourke stepped onto the coach that day determined to further drive home a point in the coming hours. He took up his window seat one row from the back and gathered his thoughts. Not only was Armagh's summer being salvaged but so was his own.

O'Rourke had always been inspired by strong characters such as Roy Keane, Richie McCaw and Nasser Hussain, the English cricketer who

Simon Barnes of the *Times* once described as 'perhaps the finest captain to hold the office'.

The Dromintee clubman was built in a similar mould. Had he not been named to start in the first Qualifier against Down, a confrontation with management was inevitable.

O'Rourke had played – and impressed – throughout the 2001 National League Division 2A campaign, mostly at corner-back, featuring in every game. He further enhanced his reputation with a starring role at centre half-back as Jordanstown defeated UCD in the Sigerson final a month before the start of the Championship.

However, when the first 15 for Armagh's Ulster clash with Tyrone was named, O'Rourke was not included. He would see only four minutes of action as they meekly surrendered their Ulster three-in-a-row ambitions to a hungry, youthful Red Hand outfit. Too much loyalty to older players was the reason he didn't start, in his view.

Against Down and Monaghan, however, O'Rourke had played all 140 minutes plus change, and he was down to start against the Tribesmen.

Unlike the gregarious Tierney, O'Rourke always looked inward before games. To be snapped out of that because of a traffic jam was simply unacceptable.

'The management tried to keep the problem away from us for as long as possible,' he says. 'There had been a good bit made in advance about arriving at Croke Park and being ready for action. We would be economical with our time; there'd be no hanging about.

'There had been chat in the lead-up to the game about players not liking being there too early, looking at the stadium. There was a feeling it wasn't great psychological preparation. At that stage we had a fair reputation that we couldn't win at Croke Park. We won Ulster titles in 1999 and 2000, and couldn't beat Meath and Kerry. We did have a name for a team that couldn't get it done in Croke Park.

'We had a big start in '99 against Meath, but the narrative was that Armagh were good enough, but would shit the togs in the Championship moments.

'We left Na Fianna knowing we were tight for time, but not behind time, but as soon as we saw the traffic, we knew it was a disaster. There were conversations on the way across and it was wondering what stage do we get off the bus and walk to Croke Park.

'I can't remember which road it was, but we were close enough and then we turned onto a street and it was just mental. There was no way we were getting through. McAlinden was on the road, the county chairman was on the road, everyone was trying to move traffic. Everyone bar the players were on the road.'

When Armagh finally reached Croke Park, the fact that they were playing in the first game only compounded matters.

The Hogan Stand was in the middle of its reconstruction and access was limited, and with Sligo and Kildare being allocated the Cusack Stand changing rooms, it meant for the first and only time at Croke Park, Armagh had to race to the other end of the ground to get ready in the cramped surroundings of a changing room under the Canal End stand.

'We were already pushing it and we weren't in the Cusack or the Hogan changing rooms, we were way down behind the Canal End in this small, pokey changing room,' says McConville. 'Of all days to be in there. I was never in it before and I've never been in it again.

'I don't know if it's what the referees use to change, but people were banging on the door, wanting us out. There was no space, and you just realise you're in serious bother. The panic has already set in and it's the case of trying to make the best of a bad situation.

'All people need to do is watch the first-half performance to realise we were a team caught like rabbits in the headlights. We were absolutely desperate, and that includes myself – I was brutal. We were living in a nightmare.'

McConville, like all the starting players, had his routine messed with, and that gnawed at him.

'As much as you were trying to deflect all those unexpected emotions, it was impossible. If there was something that used to bug me about games, it was match timings. Even now, managing my own teams, it causes me a lot of angst and a lot of nightmares.

'On that day, everything was thrown out of sync. It was a matter of getting in and getting changed as quickly as you could. Proper strapping and that sort of thing didn't happen; there was a queue waiting for the physio. Normally at that stage I would have gotten a rub on my left hamstring, but that didn't happen. That's always in your head, knowing that you're not doing what you normally do.

'We were trying to have some semblance of a warm-up and the referee just wasn't having it. It doesn't become a time thing anymore; it becomes an emotional thing. It becomes a distraction.'

As was the norm under that management, and would be in Joe Kernan's time too, captain Kieran McGeeney delivered the final stirring words of advice before the team exited the changing room.

For Aidan O'Rourke, those words of encouragement rarely registered with him. The Orchard half-back began his mental preparation for games very early, so the minutes before throw-in were an internal conversation that blocked out any external influences.

Joe Kernan's manipulation of his own memorabilia before matches to inspire his side are legendary in GAA folklore, but ask O'Rourke about the time anything was smashed off the wall and he'll draw a blank.

What he does remember is the management's attempts to get a delay to the throw-in time. The fact that the two games were to be screened live complicated matters, and in the end, referee Brian White threw the ball in just a few minutes later than he was scheduled to.

'The game was live on TV. I don't know who was doing the negotiating, but the craic was that the biggest hassle was RTÉ,' O'Rourke said. 'They were trying to move the time back, but they had a tight TV schedule.

'We had 20 minutes from arriving to get on the pitch and play. It was a scattering match in the dressing room.'

Armagh's performance in the first half spoke of a team in disarray, with Tommy Joyce's early score a case in point.

When Pádraic Joyce received possession 40 metres from goal, four Armagh players – Ger Reid, Kieran McGeeney, Paul McGrane and Andy McCann – all motioned towards him. Enda McNulty steamed out from the full-back line to meet him too.

It was schoolyard ball-chasing. It left Tommy Joyce with the simplest of kicks as his run down the right wing wasn't tracked, despite an abundance of orange jerseys in the vicinity. Before he got his shot away, McGeeney, McGrane, McCann and McNulty all tried to scamper over to him, leaving Pádraic Joyce, Jarlath 'Ja' Fallon and Kieran Comer free on the edge of the 'D'. From a coaching point of view, it was criminal.

Basic mistakes were obvious at both ends of the pitch. Oisín McConville messed up a couple of half goal chances, while John McEntee blasted over when he really should have rattled the net.

Armagh were clearly off their game and if anything, they were not punished enough for their lethargy, trailing by just four points at the interval, 0-8 to 0-4.

The cramped changing rooms at half-time offered no solutions, only more problems, and Galway continued to stroll towards the next round.

John O'Mahony's side extended their advantage in the third quarter and led 0-12 to 0-5. McConville was losing his own mental battle, while marker Kieran Fitzgerald was dominating him in the physical one.

'It felt like the quickest game I was ever involved in,' he says. 'You missed the build-up, you missed the kick-about, you missed the preparation. Until you have been there and realise the preparation that goes in, you have no idea about the actual effect that it would have on a team. The anxiety built throughout the day.

'I was a fucker at that stage for taking my time getting ready. Two pairs of socks and all that sort of thing. I used to expend as much energy putting on my socks as I did in the game.

'You are out of sync as a person, then that first half or three-quarters of the game you can see that the team is too. I found things difficult on Fitzgerald that day. I had played against him in a League match and I had a good aul' time on him, but he was good that day.'

The battle looked long lost as the game entered its final quarter, but then the momentum swung almost by stealth. Big momentum swings usually rely on a spark, but Armagh's comeback started as a trickle before eventually developing into a flood.

Sixteen minutes were left on the clock when Diarmaid Marsden raised a white flag. Armagh still trailed 0-12 to 0-6, and the point was met with muted applause.

Stevie McDonnell reduced the deficit further before substitute Cathal O'Rourke left four points between the sides with a free.

By the time Barry O'Hagan brought Armagh to within striking distance, a murmur of excitement was emanating from the large gathering of Orchard fans in the exposed, half-built Hogan Stand.

At this point, there could be no doubting that the situation had changed. Galway had been sleep-walking towards the full-time whistle, and awakening from such a slumber is always difficult in elite sport.

'There was a hole dug at half-time, but it wasn't beyond us,' says Aidan O'Rourke. 'The second half bore that out. On the pitch with 10 or 12 minutes to go, the feeling very much was that we were going to win the game. There was an inevitability about it.

'We had overrun Galway at that stage, particularly in the scrap for the ball. I had a very strong sense on the pitch that we were winning everything, winning every 50/50 ball.

'Galway's forwards were pretty impressive, and if they got enough ball up they were going to do damage, but they weren't winning enough. Our tackling was very good and we put them under serious pressure.

'I couldn't see us losing that game.'

Cathal O'Rourke stood over two more frees.

One of the most experienced players in the panel, he was the county's Player of the Year in 2000 and still had a massive role to play as an impact sub.

His free-kick routine was familiar to all who followed club football in Armagh. Four steps back, two to the right, spit over his right shoulder, a rub of the shorts and a left-footed kick off the deck that usually split the posts.

The routine helped bring Armagh back to within a point, and Galway were rocking.

His younger brother Aidan was watching from the sidelines at this stage, having been replaced by Kieran Hughes. He had extra reason for hoping that his teammates got the job done, with an error earlier in the game preying on his mind.

'I had a half-chance for a goal with about 15 minutes left, and I hesitated. At that stage, I wouldn't have been getting up the pitch too often, but I found myself 21 yards out. The natural thing for me at that time was to look for a shooter.

'It opened up and I should have driven into space and pulled the trigger. I hesitated, checked back and the covering tackle just scattered me. In the fall I did my AC joint in my shoulder. I hung on for another five minutes, but then I had to go off. I was out for a month after that.

'When you think back on games you lose, you think about your own mistakes, and that would have been a massive moment.'

It looked like O'Rourke's indecision would go unpunished, however.

In the 68th minute, Barry O'Hagan, the man who received a torrent of abuse for dropping a ball short against Kerry in the previous season's All-Ireland semi-final, brought the sides level.

There could only be one winner from here. The big question was, could Armagh win it before full-time?

Then came the moment that ensured that Armagh would exit the All-Ireland series to the eventual champions for the third season in succession.

Deep into additional time, referee Brian White was looking at his watch as Barry O'Hagan brought the ball out of his own half. With a Galway player approaching, he fist-passed to Justin McNulty on his right.

The Mullaghbawn defender generally avoided kicking the ball, but now at midfield and with excellent movement inside, he tried to deliver a pass towards the full-forward line. Instead of the ball travelling 40 metres though, Galway's Michael Donnellan stood up tall, got two hands up and blocked it down.

Quick as a flash, he gathered possession, bounced the ball and cleverly side-stepped Paul McGrane. Kieran McGeeney had read the situation and appeared to have cut off his route, but Donnellan showed a sleight of hand to fist the ball into the chest of Paul Clancy. Clancy looped around and slotted the ball between the posts, to secure a 0-13 to 0-12 win for the Connacht side.

The piece had its apparent villain, but McNulty insists he didn't receive any abuse, either inside or outside the dressing room.

'I didn't take any abuse, apart from abuse from myself,' he says. 'These moments happen in matches. In sport, and in life, you suffer setbacks and you can sit down and feel sorry for yourself or you can stand back up and get on with it. I tried to endeavour for it never to happen again.

'Listen, I was blocked down well, I saw the pass on and Donnellan blocked me down.

'In the full-back line you're more prone to being exposed to mistakes, and it happened at a stage of the match that was pivotal to the outcome. There were many more incidents of the game that were equally as important, but because they didn't happen at that juncture of the game, they didn't have the same impact.

'We didn't turn up for the first half, but my moment happened at the end of the match so people remember that. That's the way it is.'

McConville and Aidan O'Rourke take the same view.

'Justy took a good bit of stick. It was the final mistake,' McConville says. 'It looked like we had weathered the storm and weren't going to lose anyway, it was just so cruel. It just put the tin hat on what had been a disaster of a day.'

'In those last moments it did become frantic, but it shouldn't have come down to that,' O'Rourke adds. 'You look at the chances we missed over those 70 minutes and the bad decisions we made, it shouldn't have come down to that. Nobody was blaming Justy.

'Even if it had gone to a replay, I think we would have won it comfortably. By the end of the game, there was a sense that we were comfortably a better team.'

It was Galway who moved forward to round four though. Wins over Cork, Roscommon, Derry and Meath handed them their ninth All-Ireland title, ensuring the taste in Armagh mouths became even more bitter, especially as Meath in 1999 and Kerry in 2001 had gone on to lift Sam after leaving the Orchard in their wake.

The Gardaí not showing up wasn't directly the fault of the management, but that's where most of the blame was directed in the immediate aftermath, according to McConville.

'There was anger towards the two Brians. As far as you're concerned, that's their job, their remit. It didn't kick off on the bus, because there was no point at that stage. I always thought after it that if we had won that game, there would have been a massive bust-up, because there were a lot of strong characters around.

'The two Brians weren't behind the door either when it came to dishing out stick either, so there would have been a serious inquest. A lot of people thought it was the end of the road that day, after the loss anyway, there was a feeling that people on that bus would be moving on.

'It was a pretty damning day for Armagh football. As much as you can say the Guards didn't show and this and that, at the end of the day we were late. At the end of the day they were in charge of the team so, unfortunately for them, it fell back on them.

'We were doing okay and we weren't that far away, and there may have been a discussion about their future had we went on, but that Galway mess was the nail in their coffin.'

For Brian Canavan, the issues over the escort, something that was out of their control, sounds too much of an excuse.

'I don't know who would have done the organising of that, but we had nothing to do with that. They were supposed to come and take us round to the pitch and they never showed up. It wasn't the only time it happened; even in later years under Joe Kernan it happened.

'These things happen, but I didn't see it having any affect. It was only an excuse, because we were in with plenty of time. The problem was the dressing room. It was a smaller one, but we didn't pick them; Croke Park picked them.

'You get the blame, but we didn't have any role to play with the Guards or the dressing room. Galway had a similar dressing room, so they were no different. The boys who didn't play well might say that was the reason, but the reason they didn't play well was because they weren't on form. They were marking a better player or something.'

'The Guards were supposed to bring us in, but the batteries went down on their mobiles, that's what we were told,' says Brain McAlinden. 'We couldn't do anything about it, but you will get the blame. We were responsible for running late, but it was totally out of our power.'

After they got off the bus, and in the days that followed, the players met for the post-mortem in pubs across the county. The Carrickdale Hotel on the border, McKeever's in Portadown and the Golf Club in Newry were all popular haunts for the annual tradition.

Armagh could drown their sorrows with the best of them when their All-Ireland ambitions fell short for the year. There was a mood for change among the players as the drinking tour rumbled on.

The twin McEntees had already established reputations as straight-talkers. Joe Kernan was the only man for the job, they opined – and that view was strengthened by the fact that, as non-drinkers, neither could be accused of letting the alcohol talk.

It is a commonly held perception that the two Brians decided enough was enough after the game. But while McAlinden felt the juice was running very low, Canavan had different ideas.

'I was already planning for the next year,' he says.

'A man arrived at the door one night a couple of weeks later and told me they were standing us down. I asked why. He says, "We think you have taken us as far as you can." I said, "What do you mean by that?" The poor man was only sent; he had no chance. I went through what we had done.

'There was no reason for it. I said, "Are people looking Big Joe in?" He said that it had to go through the proper protocols, and I said, "Who are you trying to kid here?"

'Joe's shadow was always looming.'

Canavan was certainly on the money with that. There was only one person set to take over the side.

Opposition to 'Big Joe' was nothing more than a few names mentioned in dispatches in press reports. Donegal's Martin McHugh, Armagh man Peter Rafferty – none of them was a serious contender. Once Kernan admitted his interest, any drama was taken out of the appointment process.

On Wednesday, 29 August, Joe Kernan was confirmed as the new manager of Armagh. Things would never be the same again.

Chapter Six

More Than a Game

The shadow of Joe Kernan had been looming over Armagh football long before 2001. One of the best midfielders in the game in the 1970s and 1980s, his rewards included two All-Stars.

In the 1977 All-Ireland final, when it was clear that Dublin were simply too strong, Kernan kept the fire burning with two goals. Prior to the match, the late Donal Carroll had travelled to Crossmaglen to chat with Kernan for the *Irish Independent*. For a man who has conducted hundreds of interviews over the years, it is one that stands out for Kernan.

Chronicling the difficulties Carroll and his photographer had in locating Kernan's home, the piece describes how the pair were stopped by the British Army and had their car searched. For Kernan, it was about time the Southern press took notice of Armagh, warts and all.

After retiring, he quickly turned to coaching. He was part of Paddy Moriarty's backroom team when the Lurgan man took charge of Armagh ahead of the 1989 season.

From then until he took the Armagh job in late 2001, he would guide Crossmaglen to three All-Ireland titles, three Ulster titles, five Armagh Championships and four U21 county titles.

Everything seemed to fall into place to ensure that he would take over his beloved county and guide them to the Promised Land – with the Louth and Cavan County Boards part of the story too.

In 1997, after Paddy Kenny stepped down, Kernan was one of six people considered for the Louth job, alongside Liam Austin, Michael Heeney, John O'Leary, Eamonn Coleman and Paddy Clarke. Coleman, who had been advising the Wee County side Naomh Malachi that season, had the big one on his CV – a Sam Maguire. Kernan's résumé wasn't too shabby either at that stage, with an All-Ireland Club success arriving a few months earlier.

In the end, it was the late Paddy Clarke who got the job. He delivered an All-Ireland B title and a Division Two success in his four-year stint.

As fate would have it, former Down midfielder Liam Austin, who won an All-Star in 1983, a year after Kernan's second, would also be part of the story for Big Joe's second knockback a few months later. The Crossmaglen man was favourite to replace Martin McHugh as Cavan boss, but any hopes of a happy new year were ditched as Austin was announced on 1 January 1998.

It would prove an unhappy voyage for Austin. After a steady but unspectacular debut season, the Cavan players met and voted to remove him and his management team.

In January 1999, a year and a week on from his appointment, Austin held a press conference in Cabra Castle. He exited stage left, but not before delivering some stern words for Breffni parties who, he felt, had held him back from succeeding.

The double setback stung Kernan, but it also took his life on an entirely different path.

'A boy told me to go for the job in Louth, but there were obviously a lot smarter men in Louth than me and I didn't get the job,' says Kernan. 'I was to be nailed on for the Cavan job. A friend of mine, Ollie Brady, told me that it was mine and when I didn't get it, I said, "Ollie, you're some friend." I was after winning an All-Ireland title with Cross, but they didn't give the job to me either.

'Things are meant to happen and I am a great believer in what is meant to be. Maybe they both did me a favour.'

Subsequent events suggest that the size of that favour would be quite substantial, and it's not as if Kernan hadn't suffered before. He was, after all, from a place that was notorious in British Army circles, known by three simple letters: XMG.

On county final day 1970, Gene Duffy and Gene Larkin were part of the Crossmaglen senior panel that defeated then bogey side Clan na nGael. For the first time in the club's history, they would be doubly engaged, as their minors were also in final action on the same day. Despite Joe Kernan's presence at the centre of the pitch, his future Armagh teammate Des Mackin would rule the skies for the victorious Cullyhanna outfit.

A few months later, Duffy and Larkin sat in the former's house, where British Army personnel made it clear that rather than cede the part of Crossmaglen's pitch they had occupied as the Troubles flared up, they were considering plans to commandeer the entire plot of St Oliver Plunkett Park.

'There was a meeting held in our house and we met their civil representatives and we asked them what their full intentions were,' Duffy, who would go on to sit on councils at county, provincial and national level, said of that meeting.

'They were out to the 50-yard line at the time and I threw one out to them, I asked them had they any plans to take the entire place over.

'We said if they were, could we be given a new location adjacent to the town; that could be a solution. That was thrown out as bait – there was never any intention of us moving, but they laid out their plans on the table.

'They had plans to take over the entire pitch and there was to be a small soccer pitch in the middle of it; tennis courts too. They were showing us on the basis that they thought we were interested in moving. They wouldn't have shown us this otherwise.

'There were four of us at that meeting, including the late Gene Larkin, chairman of the club. Immediately afterwards, we rang Con Murphy, who was President of the GAA. Con drove to Dublin, arrived at Croke Park and had a meeting with Liam Mulvihill, the Director General of the GAA, about writing a letter of protest.

'We went to the British Ambassador's house that night in Ballsbridge and we had the RTÉ cameras with us. The ambassador's secretary, or whoever it was, took the letter and it was on the nine o'clock news that night.

'There was uproar. The lads who came and told us their plans, I never heard tell of them again. They let the thing slip.'

In response, the club called a town meeting and explained just how damaging it could be if the British Army were to continue their advancement.

A professor of Irish history was invited to articulate the potential conse-
quences if Cross was transformed into a garrison town.

Action, peaceful action, followed that meeting. A protest rally attended
by every club in Ulster attracted over 10,000 to the south Armagh town.

'There was a massive parade from the church car park out the Newry
Road. The main platform was at the bottom end of the ground, with the
army base behind us. The field was nearly covered with people – there were
estimations of 10,000 to 12,000 people there,' Duffy continued.

'The army was on the streets with their Saracens [armoured personnel
carriers]. People marched through them and there wasn't a word said. Con
Murphy led the parade. Gene Larkin was massive on that march too.

'We were lucky enough to come through it all, the occupation, without
losing kids, without fatalities.'

Crucially, kick-abouts on the pitch after school had disappeared, due to
the continual landing of helicopters, but that was revived on the provision
that there would be at least five adults present to act as chaperones.

Football had become a form of protest. The British Army were trying to
take away their oxygen by disruption, but the Crossmaglen community was
still finding a way to inhale and exhale.

Joe Kernan was amongst them. The same year that Gene Duffy and
Gene Larkin met British officials, he was making his Armagh debut as a
17-year-old cub.

He had really caught the eye at minor level. In a game against the Monaghan
minors in April 1971 in the Four County League – a local tournament of the
time – he ran riot. The 9-14 to 3-2 win put him right on the radar.

Seven months later, he would be back in 'Blayney for a National League
game against Monaghan. Despite the side throwing away a seven-point

lead, Kernan's high fetching was one of the highlights of the day, in front of a paltry crowd.

He would play for his county right through until 1987. In all that time, the sectarian warfare that had broken out in the North was never too far removed from his life.

'For all the kids and for everyone, we had to keep that club open,' says Kernan. 'The way we kept the club open was by playing and trying to win. We had to act as if they weren't there, even though they were there.

'It galvanised us into being very strong-minded, strong-willed. We were very determined people who weren't going to throw the towel in. Those characteristics can produce a very powerful team that knows when you have to step up, and the Championship is about stepping up.'

The constant cloud of potential violence wasn't just confined to Kernan's club commitments either.

'I remember coming home from Armagh training and I was followed one night coming from Lurgan. I was in the car on my own. That was scary.

'We broke training up then into three sections, the Lurgan boys trained in Lurgan, the Armagh boys in the city and the south Armagh boys trained in Camlough. You were stopped on the road constantly when you had GAA bags. Once again, you got immune to it; you got on with it because we loved our sport. We were making sure that we weren't going to be stopped from playing our sport.

'It stood us in good stead character-wise. It built us into very positive people. We were determined to keep it going and wanted to be successful. In fairness, the Crossmaglen story had a big part to play in the Armagh story.'

By the time Kernan was appointed Crossmaglen senior manager, after a successful stint with the club's U21s, the Troubles were winding down in the village, but they were not entirely absent.

In the 1970s across the North of Ireland, 2096 people were killed in the conflict. That number more than halved to 854 in the '80s. The 1990s saw another big drop, to 531. But that was still 531 funerals, 531 families in mourning, still a sickening number.

And in Crossmaglen, the British Army still patrolled the streets and flew in and out of that base in the corner of the club's grounds.

'Many's a training session was stopped for helicopters to land on the pitch. Games were stopped for the same. It was just pure intimidation. It was there every day,' says former Crossmaglen and Armagh goalkeeper Paul Hearty.

'Usually you had a few soldiers coming on and saying, "Get off the Gaelic Athletic Association pitch please, there is a helicopter coming." You'd start kicking balls at them; people would be taking the piss, and next thing a big helicopter would come and land on the 50-yard line. It would leave big imprints and wheels on the pitch.

'It was madness, and it happened several times to us. After 1994, that sort of stuff stopped, but in the late '80s and early '90s, it happened a lot, especially around the time they were reinforcing the barracks. They were landing in the field all the time and the pitch was in shite.'

Incidents weren't just limited to Crossmaglen, of course. Armagh training had been cancelled on numerous occasions when GAA teams were viewed as potential targets in the tit-for-tat violence of the Troubles.

Armagh goalkeeper Benny Tierney will never forget one particular night when he thought some Orchard players had been turned into loyalist bait.

'There were a couple of nights we were stopped by the UDR coming home, and I'll not tell you a word of a lie, I was shitting myself.

'There was one night in particular, we were in Armagh tracksuits and we were stopped once, and we went on to another roundabout at Craigavon and we were pulled in again at the roundabout. Seats were taken out and that sort of stuff. I just thought someone was going to come around this way and we were going to be riddled. We were held for about an hour and twenty minutes.'

Jarlath Burns also shared that trepidation when travelling to Lurgan for training. The Ulster Volunteer Force and, later, the Loyalist Volunteer Force were very active in the area. Any terrorist scouting for an easy target could have viewed a car full of south Armagh Catholics as manna from Heaven.

'That was the murder triangle – Billy Wright and all that. We had to cancel training for three or four crucial weeks at one stage,' says Burns. 'We'd get into Davitt Park in Lurgan and lock the gates. Three or four of our drivers would have stood on the terrace watching out to see if anyone was coming to shoot us.'

Back in the south of the county, and in Crossmaglen, the threat of loyalist death squads was less intense. In the last census carried out in the town, 95.42% of the population identified as Catholic. Towns and villages across the North, and in parts of Armagh, had sectarian divides often marked out by Irish tricolours and Union Jacks. South Armagh's battlefield was different.

'We weren't living cheek by jowl with the Protestant community. It was an easy narrative – us versus the Brits,' says Burns.

Football was still the escape in Cross, and it was all Oisín McConville ever knew.

'Until I was 11 years of age, as far as I was concerned, this was just the way everyone lived. This was the conditions they had. When we went on holidays, we normally went Kerry direction, and all I saw was football. We would go to Kerry training or we'd go to a League match involving Jack O'Shea.

'My Ma and Da would have that all planned, which gives you an idea of the upbringing I had – it was football, football, football. If Cross played in the Championship at the weekend, we'd still get at least four more Championship matches in – Down, Louth, Monaghan, wherever. That was growing up for me.'

Immersion in football wasn't enough to escape the realities of life in the six counties at that time though.

'I had seen things by eight and nine, as far as the Troubles were concerned, that a young lad shouldn't have seen,' McConville continued. 'I remember turning the corner at McEntee's shop and a couple of rockets coming over the top.

'My sister came into the house once. There had been a rocket attack and she threw herself into the hedge. She came home and she was stung from head to foot by nettles and she had no clue what had just happened. She was just in shock.

'There was also an incident with a bread van that was supposed to have a bomb in it and it was parked directly opposite my house.

'Every time there was a bomb, the windows came in, and we just swept up the glass and got on with it. We never talked about it. Nobody mentioned it; it was just the way it was. That had a profound effect on me later in life, but at the time it was just normal.'

Out on the streets of the town, the locals committed to a sort of omertà. If a British soldier said hello, you kept your eyes forward and you walked on.

If they asked how the match went, you shut your mouth and you ignored them. 'You don't talk to the Brits,' parents would tell their children growing up. It was an attitude that became engrained not only in Crossmaglen youngsters, but for much of the Catholic population across the North.

Outside St Oliver Plunkett Park, they became an irrelevance, but inside those grounds, the presence of occupying forces was becoming harder to ignore.

'I used to think there was a competition from them to see who could fly in the lowest. Some of the smaller helicopters were dangerously low at times,' says McConville. 'We would kick the ball over at the bottom goals and they'd puncture it and send it back. Nobody remembers how precious balls were back then. I'd go to Cross U9 training now and we could have 40 balls; back then you'd have four to do five teams.'

It would be easy to suggest that Crossmaglen's success owed to the resilience developed in those dark days. Coaches barking out instructions would regularly have to shout over the noise of helicopters taking off and landing.

While those character traits, the determination and desire, were driven home by the situation, the Crossmaglen dressing room was also laden with talent. The McConvilles, Oisín and Jim; the McEntee twins, John and Tony; Paul Hearty, Colm O'Neill and Francie Bellew; Donal Murtagh, Cathal Short; the list went on and on.

They also had a rivalry that would push them to new levels, and that was with a club eight miles over the road in Mullaghbawn.

When the parade started for the 2002 All-Ireland final, the first four players following the Artane Band for Armagh were Kieran McGeeney, Benny Tierney, Enda McNulty and finally Justin McNulty, water bottle in hand. All four men hailed from Mullaghbawn.

Justin McNulty simmers when you ask him if the Mullaghbawn portion of the Armagh story was underplayed. Crossmaglen's influence is often cited as the launch pad for the Sam Maguire assault, but on that famous September afternoon there were more players from Mullaghbawn than Crossmaglen in the first 15, even if McGeeney and Enda McNulty were playing their club football in Dublin by that stage.

A poem penned by Hugh Murphy on Mullaghbawn's contribution to 2002 is always close to McNulty's mind. He was gifted a framed version of it by the Lislea community after the Sam Maguire success.

'Curadmír – The Champions' Portion' speaks of how 'anvil steel from McGeeney came', how the McNultys were 'defenders of our hopes and dreams' and how there was 'no mightier than Benny's hand'.

'And to these four is due this day, when in these hills sits Éire's prize.'

McNulty does not intend to downplay the Crossmaglen part of the legend, but instead to amplify Mullaghbawn's role.

As well as his brother Enda, McNulty's twin brother Paul always acted as an inspiration in those early days when Mullaghbawn were breaking through. 'Having a twin, it's all you know. It's wonderful to have someone you are close to, someone you can trust without fail.

'My twin brother was an excellent footballer too; he played in the All-Ireland Minor final in '92 for Armagh. He scored a point against Meath with four men hanging out of him. It was one of the best points I've seen in Croke Park, under pressure and in the real white heat of battle.'

While Paul was playing in that 1992 final, Justin was stewing, unhappy with sitting on the bench. The experience only drove him further to succeed with his club, with the late, great Charlie Grant honing that determination into something tangible on the pitch.

'I remember my first training session with Charlie Grant, God rest him, and what a wonderful gentleman he was. He trained us, took us to matches, he drove the minibus. In those days, parents didn't drop their kids off, Charlie went round and picked up every kid from everywhere from the top of Sturgan Brae to the far side of Cashel.

'He was a man of integrity, a man that gave everyone fairness. He wanted the best for us. He was like a second father almost.

'In Armagh we won the Intermediate in 1991, and to go from winning Intermediate in '91 to the Ulster Club in '95 is a big achievement. The club went from Junior champions in 1986 to Ulster champions in '95 – that's something that's not really recognised.'

'There isn't a team in Ireland that did what Mullaghbawn did, that went from Division Four in 1985 to Ulster Club champions in 1995,' adds Benny Tierney. 'A couple of us have Division Four, Division Three, Division Two, Division One, Junior Championship, Intermediate Championship, Senior Championship, Minor Championship and U21 Championship-winning medals.'

It was as rapid a rise as you're likely to witness in Gaelic football.

Mullaghbawn's ascent through the ranks saw them back in the senior grade in 1993, chasing a first title at that level since their one and only prior success back in 1964. Joe McNulty was one of the stars of that team, and his sons were determined to emulate their father's feat.

They had sensed it was their time in 1994, but a 2-5 to 0-6 final loss to Clan na nGael stung, especially having lost to them in the semi-final the previous season. Benny Tierney was in nets; Kieran McGeeney was at six. Justin McNulty and then-Armagh star Nial Smyth were a formidable midfield partnership, while Enda McNulty came in off the bench.

Despite four points from Patrick McGeeney, brother of Kieran, the Lurgan outfit were too strong in the rain. County men Barry McCabe and John 'Soupy' Campbell both enjoyed fabulous outings in front of watching Armagh manager Jim McCorry.

When the draw was made for 1995, Mullaghbawn wanted just one thing – to be paired with Clan na nGael. Peter McDonnell, Noel Murphy, Aidan Smyth and their players had their prayers answered.

While they had Clans in the crosshairs, another side were staring down Mullaghbawn – Crossmaglen.

After gaining revenge on the Clans in that opening match with a 1-10 to 0-6 scoreline, Mullaghbawn and Cross would be paired together in the quarter-final. It was that evening that the most famous phrase in the history of Armagh club football was uttered: 'Come on the Rangers.'

BBC NI had decided to produce a fly-on-the-wall look at Gaelic games following Down's successful pursuit of an All-Ireland title in 1994. The documentary was called 'More Than a Game', and the impact of those four words, spoken by one Benny Tierney, have gone down in infamy.

The match itself was competitive and close. Mullaghbawn won 0-12 to 0-10, with Kieran McGeeney delivering a masterclass at centre half-back to help them into the last four.

Things nearly collapsed for Mullaghbawn in the semi-final, as they had to wait 24 minutes for their first score against underdogs St Peter's. With Nial Smyth in an unfamiliar position on the edge of the square, being curbed by Lenny Moore, they looked in trouble. Luckily for them, the Whites had only one point on the board by the time Mullaghbawn found the target, and the south Armagh men had made it back to the final.

The 1995 win over Armagh Harps was not a classic. Far from it. But in the horrible rain, Mullaghbawn came out on top. Fergal McDonnell lifted the Gerry Fagan Cup for the first time in the club's history – it was the McKillop Cup that had arrived back to the foot of Slieve Gullion in 1964.

Mission accomplished, but there was more to come in Ulster.

Before every game, a Mullaghbawn native would place a club flag on top of a fairy tree in the parish as the side chased down more history. It seemed to do the trick, as they got past Antrim side Cargin before taking out Monaghan heavyweights Castleblayney, kicking the last four scores to win 0-13 to 0-10 in Newry.

That set up a final with Cavan outfit Bailieboro Shamrocks in Clones. It was one of the most controversial ever finishes to an Ulster Club decider.

Mullaghbawn had been cruising, but were being reeled in and had a cushion of only three points when the Breffni side were awarded a free in. 'Last kick,' said referee Pat McEnaney. Aidan Connolly, Cavan's Player of the Year in 1995, took aim, but Benny Tierney deflected the ball onto another player. The rebound fell to Brian O'Callaghan, who dispatched to the net.

Both teams wheeled away in celebration. McEnaney ruled in favour of the Armagh side. He did say 'last kick', after all. Mullaghbawn had become only the second Orchard side to win the Ulster Club title, after Clan na nGael's three in-a-row between 1972 and '74.

An All-Ireland quarter-final in London against Tara Gaels followed, and the parish packed their bags. Due to be played in Ruislip, heavy fog and frost saw it moved to English ground Parnell Park. Tierney couldn't see past halfway with the fog, but it mattered little as the English club failed to score in the first half.

Given the game was delayed an hour, the rush was on to make the flight home to Belfast, but they got there in enough time to enjoy a few celebratory pints. The beeps of the Tannoy then chimed out, announcing that the flight had been cancelled, prompting huge cheers from the team.

A hotel was found in London and the celebrations carried on. Mullaghbawn were in an All-Ireland semi-final, a decade on from playing Division Four football in Armagh.

In February 1996, their incredible run came to an end in Navan, as Carlow outfit Éire Óg, with 12 county players in their ranks, beat them by six points. Back home in Crossmaglen, Joe Kernan didn't take much notice, but a few months later, the result would provide plenty of inspiration.

'When Mullaghbawn beat us, they went on and won an Ulster title. So when we beat them the following year, and I never mentioned Ulsters or All-Irelands until we beat Mullaghbawn and Clan na nGael to win the county title in '96, it became about bettering what they did,' says Kernan.

'I told the boys that I hadn't taken on the job to win an Armagh title, I had taken it on to win an All-Ireland. I had to tell them straight away that they had to be better than Mullaghbawn. It was no good winning an Ulster; it had to be an All-Ireland.'

There was something else providing inspiration too, and it came from that aforementioned 'More Than a Game' documentary. Beautifully capturing the emotions that accompany a big Championship game, it provided a fantastic insight into the Down, Crossmaglen and Mullaghbawn camps ahead of their dates with destiny.

The footage from the two dressing rooms in Armagh beforehand was special. Peter McDonnell was like a man possessed, rallying his Mullaghbawn troops. A few yards away, Joe Kernan wore the calm demeanour of a manager who expected nothing but victory.

'I don't care how we win boys, as long as we win,' Kernan signed off.

'One bite of the cherry; you go out there and do your job,' was McDonnell's parting shot.

At full-time, and with Mullaghbawn progressing after 60 minutes of uncompromising derby action, all the tension of the build-up was lost as the management teams and players sportingly congratulated and commiserated with each other.

When it aired on BBC months later, it would have made tough viewing for the Rangers club, given all they had put into the ultimately futile effort to beat Mullaghbawn in 1995.

One moment, however, would go down in local folklore.

With just five minutes of the programme left, the cameras cut to the Mullaghbawn clubhouse, and all that could be heard was, 'Come on the Rangers.'

The camera doesn't show who said it, but in Mullaghbawn they know. In Crossmaglen they know.

A few pints deep, Benny Tierney belts out the phrase that was viewed as a dig at Cross supporters. In Cross, the reactions differed, but the blood was up in many.

Oisín McConville laughed when he saw it; Paul Hearty didn't take it to heart either, but said it was manufactured into tangible motivation.

'Benny saying that, it was definitely something used in training to spur us on. We were so close yet so far, so anything helped. Timing is critical.'

Tierney himself felt that any suggestion that he was crucial to the success of Crossmaglen is disrespectful to everything the south Armagh club achieved in the game. 'People would say that we lit a fire in them, and me personally, that I lit a fire in them in some way as well. But you can only win an All-Ireland if you've a really good team.

'You know, you'll get through a game or two out of ignorance and out of arbitration or an enemy factor, but you won't go on to win an All-Ireland unless you're brilliant. And they were brilliant.'

That brilliance brought unprecedented success. Cross took complete control of the Armagh club scene, were dominant in Ulster and became kingpins of Ireland too. Between 1996 and 2015, the Rangers won 18 out of 19 Armagh titles. More impressively, they converted those wins into 11 provincial successes and six All-Ireland crowns.

Kernan delivered half of those All-Ireland titles from 1997 to 2000. Three Andy Merrigan Cups in four seasons was a scarcely believable achievement, and it just adds weight to the astonishing feat of Galway side Corofin completing the three-in-a-row from 2018 to 2020.

Oisín McConville thinks back to a sliding-door moment in his footballing career. This was his club's deliberations on whether or not to give Kernan and his management team of Donal McKenna and Ollie McEntee another year in 1996, after the loss to Mullaghbawn. The committee were aware of just how close the side were, and landed on the right side of history.

'It took Joe a while to get a feel for things and see how people were,' McConville says. 'That 1996 season was his fourth year, and there was a question mark about whether or not he was going to get another year. That changes history if he doesn't. That changes everything, because you just don't know where things would have gone from there.

'The next person in may have been in just for a year or two years, and then it gets all over the place. The value of giving a manager a bit of time to find his feet was crucial for us. I think at the time there was a bit of a change in standards and expectations.

'One of the things we started doing was going to Dublin for challenges. We were playing against teams who had been in All-Ireland Club finals or semi-finals. We were going there and most of the time we were winning those games convincingly. We started to feel really good about where we were. That was a mental signal that we were on a different level, but we had to prove it when we played.

'We only beat Sarsfields by a point in the first round, and that was such an important day for the club. Lose that and Joe's gone, no doubt. That's the fine margin.'

That Sarsfields game was the opener to the 1996 Armagh Championship season. It would be the first in a seemingly never-ending list of tight contests salvaged by the men in black-and-amber.

In that dream run from 1996 to 2016, starting with that 0-9 to 2-2 win over Sarsfields and ending with a one-point All-Ireland semi-final loss to Castlebar in February 2016, Crossmaglen won 11 replays and lost only one. That was to Errigal Ciaran in 2002, when their second meeting ended all square after extra-time as well. Their 2015 Ulster title also came via an extra-time win, over Scotstown.

On top of that, the period brought another 12 one-point victories after that Sarsfields success, helping to create an incredible mystique status. The club was drawing admiring glances from across the country. Various Cross management teams were happy for that to be portrayed by friends in the media. It all added to the awe.

Journalists loved coming to St Oliver Plunkett Park for media nights or to cover the Rangers. From Margaret McConville you were guaranteed one of the warmest welcomes in Ulster. For all the club's successes in the men's game, she is one of the most revered figures associated with the club.

Crossmaglen were a special side, but their success did not come from some special characteristics unique to them. Two key factors stand out. Firstly, they were incredibly talented, having won four Armagh U21 titles leading into that period of dominance. Secondly, they worked like absolute demons on the pitch.

Perhaps youth was also an important attribute, giving that ability to come strong at the death. In their first All-Ireland win in March 1997, only Jim McConville was over the age of 30.

The diminutive attacker was also the only player with a county medal in his pocket before that season, having been involved in their previous county triumph in 1986.

'I remember that one in '86,' Paul Hearty says. 'I don't remember the football, and I wouldn't have been at any of the matches, but I remember Jim McConville at the top of a white Moley's bus with the McKillop Cup, as the title was then.

'They went around the town and we all ran down from the park to see what was going on. I was in awe of these boys going around, the flags out and the horns beeping and Jim, only a pup at the time, with the cup. It was magical to me. Stars in your eyes sort of thing.'

One of the greatest strengths of Cross was the ability to get their key men fit and ready for Championship football year after year. Oisín McConville was an ever-present. You rarely saw the McEntees missing a game.

They could have been down Francie Bellew for the start of the 1998 campaign though, had Hearty and his jet ski inflicted any more damage in America. 'We rented jet skis in Florida after we won the All-Ireland in 1997,' says the goalkeeper. 'It was someone's bright idea to take a lock of lads who had never been on jet skis before, nor hardly knew what they looked like, out onto the Everglades, with probably crocodiles all over the place.

'I was flying about as a young lad and trying to steer and trying to go faster. I found myself on a head-on course with Francie Bellew. I stupidly didn't know that you had to put the power on for steering, so I had it off and was trying to turn and it wouldn't turn.

'Francie came straight for me and into the yoke and we ended up ploughed into each other. We were alright though; we just had a bit of a bill to pay for the damage.'

On the same day in September 1996 as Crossmaglen eased past Clan na nGael in the Armagh final to end their long wait for a county title, John 'Shorty' Treanor became Ulster's most decorated club footballer, winning a ninth club title with Down side Burren.

It was an astonishing achievement, elevated further still when he broke into double figures in 1997. Just over a decade later, a raft of Crossmaglen footballers would overtake his haul.

Mullaghbawn's footballers had scaled real heights before Crossmaglen outdid them. That silver-laden rivalry was fierce. And the real winners would be Armagh. Joe Kernan was Commander-in-Chief for the Rangers during their run to the top, and now he was about to try to repeat the trick for his county.

Chapter Seven

Lourdes or La Manga

Every Christmas morning during their Armagh days, Mullagh-bawn clubmen Kieran McGeeney, Justin McNulty and Enda McNulty would meet at the foot of Slieve Gullion mountain. They would look up at the rising path and start sprinting.

Up the trail, three pockets of frozen breath following like smoke rising to the sky. Up the mountain. Whatever it takes. Got to get to the top of the mountain.

When new Armagh manager Joe Kernan called his new squad to the Canal Court for the first team meeting in late 2001, he already had the room.

'I remember immediately after the Galway game, the two Brians were gone and Oisín [McConville] and the twins [McEntees] were very adamant that Joe was coming in,' says Aidan O'Rourke. 'It wasn't my business; I was a peripheral player and happy enough to be having conversations over pints, but that goes into the court of Geezer [McGeeney] and Floppy [Paul McGrane].

'The dynamic of it was that I knew the senior players were working for Joe to take over. I'm not sure that was the case with everyone at the county board, but there definitely was a sense that it had to be done right. There was talk that if the county board went on a different tangent, there could be an issue with the players.'

Kernan's principles were pretty basic. Aim as high as you can, and make sure your players have everything they could possibly need.

His backroom team would reflect that. In all, from liaison officer – and team fixer – Eamon Mackle to famed kitman Paddy 'the Bishop' McNamee, the set-up would include 16 people. Normal now, bloated back then.

A lesser-known but vitally important team member was analyst Darren O'Neill, whose background lay more in basketball than football. The Belfast man was ahead of his time, providing statistical information that was beyond the comprehension of some county teams at the time.

One such item that the management used to scrutinise on a Monday night in the Armagh City Hotel was O'Neill's version of heatmaps, marked out by hand with pen and paper. Orchard players and opposition were charted out – where they tended to shoot from; what part of the pitch they started their runs from; where they could be exposed defensively.

A number of other people had turned down invitations to join the team before the manager completed the set. Hugh Campbell and Des Jennings, who covered the psychology and sports performance side of things, linked up later in the season.

The most important two, outside of Kernan of course, were assistant manager Paul Grimley and trainer John McCloskey.

The latter had achieved great success with Crossmaglen at club level and Queen's at university level and, again, he was brought in because he could bring something different. As well as physical preparation, he worked to improve the team's skills base, both individually and collectively – tackling, shooting, passing, eye-to-hand coordination, vision, balance and speed. Every facet of the game was studied with a view to improvement. The players bought in 100 per cent.

Grimley would develop an amazing bond with the Orchard players. He would often have to deliver the devastating news to a player on the Thursday before a Championship game that they had been dropped. What should have been a thorny task would end with player and coach embracing, the pair almost on the verge of tears.

When Kernan first contacted Grimley to come on board, the response was lukewarm. Other commitments meant that he was unlikely to be able to give the time required, but Kernan got him over the line.

Once he was in, he was all in though. Grimley was never a man to shirk a challenge. Headstrong and determined, his character had been chiselled by experiences on the field, not least in the decision to move from his club Armagh Harps to their bitter city rivals Pearse Óg. In the 1985 Armagh final, Grimley picked up the Man of the Match award as the Ógs beat a Harps team containing his brothers Mark, John and Kieran.

When Kernan phoned John McCloskey in September 2001 and asked him would he help him win Sam, the trainer asked if Joe really believed that Armagh could do it. A meeting in Lurgan with Kernan and Grimley quickly put to bed any doubts McCloskey might have had.

McCloskey had worked with the Crossmaglen contingent at club level, as well as some of the others at Queen's, so they knew what to expect, especially when it came to diet. Paddy Carolan had been tasked with preparing meals after Armagh training and any chance of a wee sweet treat to finish off the refuelling was strictly off the menu.

Oisín McConville remembers the pure joylessness of having lunch with McCloskey when the pair were working together in Belfast as the player worked through a back injury. 'You're going for something to eat with him in Belfast and he's leaving stuff back because there was a touch of mayonnaise on it. I used to get a sandwich and he'd be looking through it to see what was wrong with it.

'I was in the pool in Queen's, and I could do two and half hours of aqua jogging. Twenty minutes in there, out to do exercises at side of the pool and people looking at you, and then back in. I used to do aqua jogging in Monaghan before work. McCloskey didn't trust me to do it, so I had to go see him all the time in Belfast to do it.'

There were a couple more crucial phone calls to be made before the squad came together. One was to Benny Tierney, who had been left broken after the 2001 season.

The defeat to Galway had been hard to stomach. In truth, the entire Qualifier run had been tough for the Mullaghbawn man. Tierney was in goals for the Ulster Championship loss to Tyrone, but was told that Paul Hearty would be starting the county's first-ever Qualifier against Down.

Tierney was furious and left training early upon hearing the news. He calmed down though and was there to put Hearty through his paces in the warm-up at Casement Park.

'I'm not proud of that reaction. There were other better players than me who were dropped over the years, but I think it was the first time I had ever been dropped. I think it was the sense that I didn't see it coming.'

The full-time whistle against Galway brought the curtain down not only on Armagh's season, but on his own long county career. Or so he thought.

Another call saw Kernan reach out to Crossmaglen defender Francie Bellew, who would go on to achieve cult hero status among Orchard supporters – so much so that people spoke about him using only his first name.

Tierney and Bellew had battled it out on the club scene for years as Cross and Mullaghbawn went toe-to-toe. They came into direct contact on the field too at one stage.

'I remember coming on one night and marking Francie against Cross,' Tierney says. 'They took me out of goals for the last ten minutes, there was only a couple of points in it.

'I never touched the ball like, but I met Francie a couple of years later. He said he near shit himself from fear of Tierney getting a goal off him. He said it was the most uncomfortable ten minutes he ever had in his life. Just because of what maybe I would have done after it – I probably would have done a Joe Brolly and ran round the field blowing kisses.'

Tierney's commitment to the cause had been worn down, and thoughts of a return initially left him cold. But Kernan's powers of persuasion during a meal shortly after that first Canal Court meeting convinced the goalkeeper to return.

'I knew behind the players were the women. I had to get the women onside, so I had the craic with them one evening,' says Kernan. 'We went out for a meal, and I sent the boys away for a drink so I could talk to the girls. I told them that I thought we could win the All-Ireland and it was important that they enjoy the journey too. I told them we knew the sacrifices they were going to have to make too. We wanted them to be part of it and they all bought into it.

'That's how I got Benny back; I wouldn't have gotten Benny back only for Nicola. "Her indoors", as he calls her.'

At that first meeting, Kernan delivered one key message: 'We will win the All-Ireland this year.'

Belief had been shaken by the Galway loss a few months earlier. Many outside the camp predicted the end of the road for Armagh, and this feeling had seeped through to some of the players. Doubts existed.

Three players who remained steadfast in their belief that they would win an All-Ireland were Kieran McGeeney, Enda McNulty and Justin McNulty. Up to the top of the mountain, whatever it takes.

One person at the team meeting who had none of that baggage was Annaghmore's Shane Smyth. Residing now in Kerry, he represents the other side of that Armagh 2002 squad. The fringe player, the person who doesn't get recognised walking down the street.

'I was coming into it as a complete novice; county football to Annaghmore was a no-no. I think Sammy McNeice in the '70s was the last one before me. We were fourth division at the time. We had a decent enough team at that level, but it seemed a long way off county.

'I marked Francie Bellew in the trials. I never got a ball against Francie. I'd win the ball, but he had a deadly habit of getting the hand in. He was no genius in taking you on and beating you, but he was always able to get that hand in. He made things very, very awkward.

'The first 60 minutes, I was doing centre half-forward and Francie was doing centre half-back, and then I was onto Sean O'Hare. Nice fella, good footballer, but I got the run on him and scored a goal and two points. I'd say that swung it more than anything else.

'Joe rang me that evening and I thought it was some of the boys fucking about. He said to come into the panel, and I said, "Aye, I will surely," joking about. Joe had to convince me then that it was real.'

He may have a Celtic Cross in his back pocket, but Smyth only spent one year on the Armagh panel, and only actually played one game for his county.

'Joe was under pressure, it was the first year in. He wanted to lay down a marker and he was playing a fairly strong League team. Under the Brians, six or eight lads would have been brought in and they were allowed to play together in the League, but Joe was picking a fairly strong team with a couple of newer lads mixed in.

'Joe's big thing at that stage was putting Francie into centre half-back. People were saying to me, "This is fucking mental." Kieran McGeeney was a third midfielder because of it, starting corner-forward and coming out. I'd be going back to the club and people would be asking what Joe was at.'

Smyth was happy to chat with lads at the club about Francie Bellew and Kieran McGeeney and what the new manager was trying. But he wanted to be able to chat about his own performances as well, and that conversation was on the horizon.

'We were meant to be playing Limerick late in the League and I was pretty much told that I would be starting. We were training at Callanbridge and I went for the ball and went over on my ankle and tore ligaments. Colm O'Neill came down on top of me and you could imagine the weight of big Colm. It was a pure accident. I tried to start running again after about two weeks but I never should have, because I had done serious damage to ligaments.

'I was out the whole League. I was kind of back for the London game in Ruislip. Paul Grimley said, "Do you want to go on?" but my ankle still wasn't right.

'That was my chance in terms of getting in. Big Colm told me that Joe has 16, 17 boys and he rarely goes outside of that. That scuppered me on the League front.'

Smyth's analysis holds up. In Kernan's first National League game against Louth, switched from the Athletic Grounds to Carrickcruppen late on, 11 of the 15 that started in that year's All-Ireland final would be in the line-up. Of the other four, Tony McEntee and Barry O'Hagan came on against Kerry at Croke Park, with John Donaldson and Simon Maxwell the other two.

Kernan's reign looked like it would get off to a losing start as they trailed 0-12 to 0-6 to the Wee County with 20-odd minutes left, but Stevie McDonnell took over to turn the tide.

Wicklow and Antrim were dismissed on the road, with Leitrim and Limerick downed at home. Five wins from five, with McDonnell taking his goal tally to an incredible seven.

Their first taste of defeat would come in Tralee in round six as, despite another McDonnell goal and one from Paddy McKeever, Kerry prevailed by a point. 'The next time we meet them, it will be an All-Ireland final,' Paul Grimley told the changing room afterwards.

Four first-half goals in Ruislip against London ensured top spot in Division 2A and a second-tier semi-final with Laois. Cathal O'Rourke was making his first appearance of the season, having been injured. He helped himself to 11 points, while McDonnell made it nine goals for the campaign.

With 17 goals nabbed already, and with Laois only reaching the last four due to Wexford messing up their final game against lowly Carlow, Armagh were red-hot favourites.

What followed in Longford was dour. Their hitherto lethal attack was held to just 0-8, while Laois scored 0-12. With Kerry beating Meath in the other semi-final, Paul Grimley's post-match comment in Tralee about not meeting Kerry until the All-Ireland final would come true.

When asked post-match where his side had fallen down, Kernan responded, 'From one to 15.'

This wasn't just a sound bite for the waiting press. The Armagh staff was disgusted by the performance, but it proved a loss that would alter the trajectory of their careers.

Earlier that year, John McCloskey had mentioned to Kernan the idea of a warm-weather training camp for the squad, while also pointing out the risk of ridicule that it would bring. After the Laois debacle, the manager gave him the green light to dig further.

In 2009, Mike McGurn was part of Paddy O'Rourke's Armagh back-room team as strength and conditioning coach, but in 2002 he was working with the Irish rugby team. Given that Armagh wanted to emulate a professional training week, McCloskey asked him for a recommendation. The answer came back: La Manga.

On 2 May, prior to their Ulster opener against Tyrone, the Armagh squad jetted off to Spain for an infamous training camp, knowing they were breaking new ground. At the back of Kernan's mind, and no doubt some of the players', was the thought, 'If we lose to Tyrone after this, the slagging we'll get.'

McCloskey was serene. As far as he was concerned, the squad would get five days of brilliant training two weeks out from the clash with the Red Hands.

Aidan O'Rourke was another who wouldn't be too concerned by what those outside the changing room thought. 'It was a steady thing with Joe, he steadily pressed us at various stages. Joe didn't do anything revolutionary, and he'd tell you this himself, but everything was done so professionally.

'I would imagine Joe sat and thought, "How would Man United do this?" or, "How would Leinster Rugby do this?" That's how he went about everything. That's about the environment, about training; getting training kit was fucking unbelievable. What you had to wear. Wee touches. Joe did everything brilliantly.

'Eamon Mackle, Joe's fixer, had a lot to do with that too. Eamon was always whispering, "Is there anything anyone needs?" and asking Geezer and Floppy what does anyone need. La Manga was another example of that professional touch.'

Oisín McConville wasn't exactly concerned about the fall-out either. 'It did leave us open, but at the same time, what really was there for us to lose? Because as far as people were concerned, we were a bunch of losers anyway. We were failures; we would choke in the big situations.

'As a pundit today, I would have had a field day with Armagh. Not in a cruel way, but just realism.

'La Manga plugged us all in. It was tough; it was a four-week block of training in five or six days. We trained two or three times a day.

'There was a central place and then a few bedrooms. I think I roomed with Justy McNulty for the first while – absolute nightmare. Three times a day wasn't enough for Justy; he would have gone to the gym again if he was allowed, whereas I wanted to chill out, relax.'

'I was with Pauric Duffy, and the staff in the hotel thought we were a big football team,' says Shane Smyth. 'They could hear us calling him Duff and they thought it was Damian Duff, but they weren't getting the tips that Damian Duff would have been giving.

'It was your three-a-day sessions. It might have been a gym in the morning or a field session and then maybe video analysis of Tyrone later. Now that's standard, but back then it wasn't.

'Jerome Quinn did an article about how Armagh should have gone to Lourdes, and Joe put it up on the wall before the match, saying, "Do you want to be a laughing stock if you don't win it?"'

One interesting nugget to emerge from La Manga, and one that perhaps gave Joe Kernan full faith in Paddy McKeever as a free-kick taker, was the assessment of performance coach Dave Alred. Alred specialised in kicking. Just a few months earlier, he had spent two days with Jonny Wilkinson at a soccer centre in Middlesbrough, to create the famous crouching routine that would become synonymous with England's 2003 Rugby World Cup win.

Kernan invited him to join them in Spain, and Alred spent time working with McKeever, Oisín McConville and Cathal O'Rourke. When Alred broke it all down, he judged that the Ballyhegan man's routine was a thing of beauty.

McConville, by contrast, was told that his style was too forced and cumbersome. The player opted against making any big changes, but he did take two steps off his longer free-kick routine.

Kernan hoped that these minor touches would make a major impact. La Manga became a running joke on the outside, but Armagh had to hold their nerve. It had been a brilliant camp and, for John Toal, it brought an already tightknit squad even closer.

'There wasn't a mouthful of drink taken, but there was nobody interested in it anyway,' said Toal. 'Everyone knew that we were going places and things were being done right, the management were doing everything right.

'We all had one common goal and we all believed that we could achieve it. We had a meeting one time in La Manga and I remember John McEntee got up and spoke and the hairs were standing on the back of my neck.

'I remember getting off the bus when we landed home and I was going back to Belfast with Aidan O'Rourke. I said, "We are in some shape here, we're going to beat these Tyrone boys." Aidan looked at me and said, "What are you talking about?" I said, "I think we'll beat them," and he said, "We're not going to just beat these boys, we're going to win the All-Ireland."

'It was the first time it had been mentioned. I probably didn't respond, but I remember just thinking that he was right.'

Chapter Eight

Marching Towards the Sam

While Armagh had been dreaming of All-Ireland glory under Spanish skies alongside experts in various sporting fields, the Tyrone players were back with their clubs, sharpening their weapons in the crisper spring surroundings. The Armagh game was a fortnight away, but a round of Tyrone Club Championship fixtures were pencilled in regardless.

Stephen O'Neill kicked two points for Clan na nGael as they defeated Loughmacrory. Peter Ward pulled off a smart save from Cookstown's Fergal Coyle as Dromore progressed. Ger Cavlan had an absolute stormer as 14-man Dungannon dumped out Strabane.

Art McRory and Eugene McKenna's side entered the Clones arena in good nick. Confident too.

Tyrone had hammered Mayo and Cavan in the knock-out stages to claim the Division One title. Despite delaying their team announcement to check on some niggles, Ryan McMenamin, Brian Dooher and Ciaran Gourley were passed fit to start.

The first half of the Armagh and Tyrone Ulster quarter-final was an indication of what was to come – not only in that match and the subsequent replay, but also over the course of the next four seasons in one of the great GAA rivalries.

'Any game you played against Tyrone, there was an intense rivalry and a hatred that brought both teams to new levels. It brought Gaelic games to new levels at that particular time,' says Stevie McDonnell.

'There was a real bitterness, not only between the players, but between the supporters too. That was brilliant. We knew we brought them to new levels; they knew they brought us to new levels. Only for that rivalry, who knows where those teams would have been? You look at Dublin and Meath in the early '90s; Armagh and Tyrone is up there in terms of the greatest rivalry.'

Twelve scores were evenly shared in that first half, and at no stage did either side have an advantage of more than a point.

The needle that would dominate the rivalry was evident too. When Oisín McConville scored Armagh's second point in the 11th minute, he gave Brian Dooher a flick of his elbow, the Red Hand player shoving him in response.

In McConville's 2007 autobiography *The Gambler*, he outlined the issues he had with some Tyrone players, particularly Ryan McMenamin and Conor Gormley.

The trio had clashed, McConville claimed, in a National League game in 2001, during which McMenamin spent the entire game talking about his mother and sister with Gormley joining in on the verbals too.

'I lost it that day and I punched Gormley in that mouthpiece of his and he started bleeding,' McConville wrote in his book. 'Pat McEnaney was refereeing but there were two umpires there who I am convinced saw just about everything that had happened and what I had done but never said a thing, maybe because they'd heard a lot of what they were saying.'

Tensions have eased considerably in the intervening years.

'I've met both of them since,' he says. 'Conor Gormley is someone I haven't met as much. He wouldn't be floating in the same circles as myself, but I met him and his Da in Newry one night and it passed off without incident. It seemed grand.

'Ricey [McMenamin] and I have definitely buried the hatchet – not in his head I should add – and we have moved on.'

Back at Clones, the temperature was continuing to rise and certain Tyrone players were causing Joe Kernan's side real issues. Powerful youngster Sean Cavanagh was making a real mark on the game, while the marauding McMenamin got forward to put the Ulster holders back in front at the start of the second half.

By that stage, the Armagh manager had made two substitutions that would have huge implications for the rest of the season. Towards the end of the half, Tony McEntee picked up an injury and Kernan turned to 19-year-old Ronan Clarke, who had been brought into the panel the previous year.

'Clarkie came out of nowhere,' says Stevie McDonnell. 'Clarkie wasn't showing any form. He was going to take a year or two to find his feet and find his rhythm, but out of nowhere Joe sprung him from the bench. I remember looking and thinking, this is a big call. Joe had obviously seen a bit more from him than I had.'

Paul McCormack had started the first half solidly enough, but Kevin Hughes was starting to get a run on him towards the interval. At the break, Francie Bellew came onto the pitch for his first minutes of inter-county championship action.

The game continued along a familiar path. Armagh, buoyed by the brilliant Oisín McConville, eked out a two-point lead in the 43rd minute, but Tyrone hit the next two scores, making it 0-10 to 0-10.

Then, with 49 minutes on the clock, John Toal played a swerving, floaty ball onto the edge of the square from midfield. McDonnell showed great handling to field the ball in front of full-back Brian Robinson, before finishing expertly past Peter Ward.

'Catching and playing off both sides played a big part in my game,' says the Killeavy man. 'When I first came into the Armagh set-up, I was very, very light. You're training against extremely strong players. We were renowned for being a big, physical team, and I was the slightest of them all.

'The one thing I had to learn and learn fast was to get stuck in and learn to win a dirty ball and hold onto it. Having the ability to turn out left and right definitely was of huge benefit to me. No matter what weight I was or how strong I was, it was a huge help. It was coached into me from a young age.'

In a game of such fine margins, it should have been the starter gun on a famous Ulster win, especially when Ronan Clarke tagged on a point to put Armagh four ahead. But Kernan's side did something that he would demand they never do again – they took their foot off Tyrone's throat.

His Crossmaglen side were famed for being ruthless down the stretch, but they failed to kill off the Anglo Celt holders.

Armagh still led by three late on, after a sensational Clarke point announced his arrival on the big stage. Aidan O'Rourke played a ball towards him alongside the sideline. Showing deft hands to collect possession close to the ground, he bullied Chris Lawn to the ground with ease and sliced over a beautiful effort. The reserved fist pump was that of a man who thought he'd put the seal on victory.

But there would be one more Tyrone sting, and it came courtesy of two of their best players on the day. Ryan McMenamin advanced up the wing and kicked a ball towards the Armagh goal, where Sean Cavanagh fielded the ball cleanly in front of Francie Bellew. Through a mesh of bodies, he somehow found the bottom corner of the net, with Benny Tierney scampering across goal in a futile attempt to stop it.

Tierney was stamping the ground in frustration as the ball rolled in, but was all smiles moments later as he hugged a bare-chested Peter Canavan. No matter the intensity of the battle, these two college friends would always have time for each other.

More likely though, Tierney's anger had been soothed by the gilt-edged chance to win it at the death that Tyrone spurned after their levelling goal.

Canavan had snagged a loose ball around the middle of the park and delivered a silky dummy solo to side-step Bellew before dancing past Enda McNulty. That left essentially a three on one. Ninety-nine times out of 100, Canavan would have taken four steps forward and tapped it over the bar for the win. On this occasion however, he fisted it to the free Richie Thornton, who screwed wide under pressure from the advancing Tierney and the recovering Bellew.

Kernan was bullish when he spoke after the draw, despite being pegged back so late on. He took aim at those who reckoned Armagh were done, suggesting the Orchard had proven those doubters wrong.

The draw was never going to do that, but their performance in the replay added weight to his claim.

The 'Sunday Game' cameras were not due to be back at St Tiernach's Park for the second game, but heavy rain forced the postponement of Donegal and Down in Ballybofey and Armagh–Tyrone was a late replacement on RTÉ. Few would have complained pre-match, and certainly not after, following another blood-and-thunder classic.

'A lot of people were saying RTÉ should have been showing this game anyway,' Colm O'Rourke opined on 'The Sunday Game'.

Fellow pundit Tommy Carr suggested that the commonly held belief that Oisín McConville doesn't deliver on the big day was a harsh one. It couldn't have been too common, given that the Crossmaglen man was considered one of the greatest clutch-moment players in the game. This occasion would only enhance that reputation in the years to come.

Canavan didn't get the chance to make up for his poor decision-making at the end of the first game, as a leg injury kept the Errigal Ciaran legend out of the return. The late Cormac McAnallen wore the captain's armband in his absence, while Philip Jordan, who would become a hate figure for Orchard fans a year later, made his championship debut.

For Armagh, Ronan Clarke and Francie Bellew had earned starting spots off their cameos in the drawn encounter – and this starting 15 would be the one to start against Kerry at Croke Park in the final game of the 2002 championship.

A substitute would steal the headlines though, as the blonde bombshell Barry Duffy, locks now fully regrown after the shaving incident that accompanied his debut at the same venue five years earlier, scored the goal that eventually broke Tyrone's resistance.

The opening exchanges were hard-hitting and demanding as the Red Hands, often regarded as physically less imposing than Armagh, tried to impose themselves in that particular department early on.

Collie Holmes, who was playing his club football with Armagh Harps at the time, picked up a yellow card in the third minute for a welcome challenge on youngster – and club rival – Ronan Clarke. Ryan McMenamin extended the welcome with a few choice words for the stricken Pearse Óg player, but John McEntee and John Toal arrived to clear the Dromore man out.

Gerard Cavlan also picked up a yellow card, as Paddy McKeever waited to kick the resulting free, for a hit on Kieran McGeeney. Once issued, Aidan O'Rourke met him with a few shoulders to redress the balance.

McKeever landed the free and then a second moments later, and when Clarke fisted over in the sixth minute, the game appeared to be veering away from the drawn encounter.

Any thoughts that Armagh were going to run away with it were extinguished in a blistering 10-minute spell, as Tyrone grabbed half a dozen points without reply – just after Kevin Hughes had picked up their third yellow card inside the opening seven minutes.

Following a shaky start under a barrage of long ball, Brian Robinson and Chris Lawn were firming things up in the full-back line. After ten minutes of being bullied by Paul McGrane, Cormac McAnallen was getting a foothold in the centre. Having been absent in the opening skirmishes, Brian Dooher and Kevin Hughes were now getting on a mountain of ball around midfield. Tyrone were rampant.

The second quarter belonged to the men in orange though, as the pendulum swung wildly once again. From there until the break, they would outscore their opponents 1-5 to no score, to lead by five points at the interval.

In the six legendary Championship clashes between the counties from 2002 to 2005, this was one of only two times that one of the sides held a five-point advantage.

The introduction of Kieran Hughes for Andrew McCann brought instant results. Hughes broke through three Tyrone players before finding Paul McGrane, who delivered long for Diarmaid Marsden to get Joe Kernan's side back on the scoring track.

Aidan O'Rourke then broke forward well and was fouled. Paddy McKeever, looking confident after Dave Alred's advice in La Manga, landed his third free. Oisín McConville, anonymous to that point, then brilliantly won and converted a free from close range.

By this stage, Kieran McGeeney was delivering a defensive masterclass and he linked up brilliantly with Paddy McKeever to set up a super John McEntee score. McConville landed another close-in free before the first goal of the game arrived, on the cusp of the half-time whistle.

McGrane, his Ballyhegan clubmate McKeever and O'Rourke all synchronised well to release Hughes down the wing. The early sub then fisted in-field to John McEntee, who took a bounce and produced a daisy-cutter low finish past Peter Ward.

It felt significant. McDonnell celebrated wildly in the goal. Hughes, Clarke and McConville all ran and hugged the goal-scorer. Half-time: Armagh 1-8 Tyrone 0-6.

The cameras panned to a downtrodden Peter Canavan as the teams headed off for the dressing room. Listed amongst the substitutes, a miracle from the bench seemed a requirement. A Canavan would come in off the bench that day, his brother Pascal, but in the second half his teammates showed that they were no one-man team.

Stevie O'Neill hit two quick scores on the resumption, one off each foot, to make the gap more manageable. When Kevin Hughes landed a monster score, a red-and-white momentum shift was under way.

Paddy McKeever provided some relief with another beautiful free out on the wing, but back Tyrone came, with scores from O'Neill and Cormac McAnallen. The decibels rose further at St Tiernach's Park, with just one point now between the sides and plenty of time still left on the clock.

Peter Ward denied McConville with a fine stop, O'Rourke screwing a simple pointed chance wide from the rebound, before McEntee was off target from a good position. Armagh were famed for not killing teams off and, here in Clones, they were living up to their reputation.

The settling influence was John Toal, who set up two scores in a row for McDonnell. The Keady midfielder would have been a contender for Man of the Match only for the sheer excellence McGeeney demonstrated.

Tyrone were not going to surrender their Ulster title easily though. O'Neill, Declan McCrossan and Brian McGuigan brought them level for the 13th and final time over the two games. With Peter Canavan going through a vigorous warm-up, the scene was set for another telling intervention from perhaps the greatest forward to ever play the game.

Another attacker would grab the headlines though: big Barry Duffy.

Toal had another massive part to play. In the middle of a swarm of bodies, he somehow found the space to play a clever pass forward towards McConville. Duffy took a step towards his teammate, ensuring his marker Chris Lawn had to engage, before peeling off behind him.

With three men around him, McConville got the ball back to Duffy and he squeezed the ball past Peter Ward.

'It all happens very quickly in games like that,' says Duffy. 'I just remember Oisín winning it and laying it off; he sort of drew in Chris Lawn, which gave me a bit of space. I got the ball, turned, and the Tyrone keeper was on top of me very quickly, so I just managed to place it in the bottom corner. I emphasise "place", not "miskick"! I was just glad to see it go in, and we kicked a point right after that. That gave us a four-point cushion, which maybe doesn't sound like much, but when you're playing Tyrone, even one or two points is a big, big difference.'

McKeever and McDonnell added further hammer-blows after Duffy's goal and, for the final time in the peak of their rivalry, a side would move five points clear. It would be enough this time.

Ryan McMenamin and Sean Cavanagh went close to goals, but had to settle for points, as Joe Kernan's side earned a 2-13 to 0-16 win. Psychologically, given Galway, given La Manga, given the punishment that would have followed in defeat, it was a huge victory.

They had entered the set of games as underdogs and dumped out the Ulster champions. Any suggestion that they were over the hill was finally being eroded. Benny Tierney greeted the full-time whistle by dropping to his knees and raising his hands to the skies, before slamming them into the ground three times. Team captain Kieran McGeeney headed to the sideline to embrace Tony McEntee, who was on crutches from the injury he had picked up in the draw.

'You saw the reaction of Brendan Tierney, the Armagh goalkeeper, at the end of the game – you'd think they'd won the All-Ireland,' Michael Lyster said back in the 'Sunday Game' studio.

'They [the Armagh players] know what I think of them; it's the rest of the country I was worrying about these last few weeks – they were writing them off,' Joe Kernan said afterwards.

Given what they had put into those two games, Fermanagh were essentially no-hopers in the Ulster semi-final. The 1990s had witnessed many Ulster Championship meetings between the sides and the general trend was that Armagh would grind out narrow victories.

The Fermanagh faithful still had nightmares about their 1993 preliminary round replay clash at the Athletic Grounds. Armagh had escaped with a draw from Irvinestown thanks to a late point from captain John Rafferty, but it seemed to be all for nothing, as the Erne County led by nine points with just five minutes remaining in the second match.

From there, Armagh would hit an incredible 3-2, with Denis Hollywood grabbing two of those goals and John Grimley coming forward to fire past Cormac McAdam for Armagh's most incredible championship victory.

Afterwards, Tierney consoled McAdam, and the two remain close friends to this day. In 2006, McAdam was left paralysed from the waist down after falling from a roof while plastering a chimney. Since then, and with the help of a motorised buggy, he has become a fine golfer, so it's no wonder Tierney – fond of the fairways himself – has kept in contact.

While their 1990 clashes were tight affairs, by 2002, Armagh were operating on a completely different plane to Fermanagh. The difference in class was evident as they romped to a 0-16 to 1-5 win. In Orchard Harvest, the DVD released to celebrate Armagh's heroic season, the editing team opted against showing any highlights from the first half.

Even when that first half concluded with Armagh just a point to the good, there was a sense of inevitability about the outcome, especially as the Erne County had played with a significant breeze.

Fermanagh didn't score from the 14th minute until a 1-1 salvo from Rory Gallagher in additional time put a bit of respectability on the score-line. It was men against boys. A pretty perfect day for Armagh, although Shane Smyth wasn't sharing in the joy.

In the 55th minute, Cathal O'Rourke was summoned from the bench to replace Paddy McKeever. The experienced Dromintee man scored a point, but picked up an injury late on.

'There was one match in particular that it was made clear that you weren't going to feature, and then you didn't really enjoy it,' Smyth says. 'It was the Fermanagh game. Paddy McKeever was doing alright, but he was taken off and they brought on Cathal O'Rourke. Cathal was injured and I was the only other option left, but they put Paddy back on.

'There were only a few minutes to go and the game was won, and Paddy scored a point so you couldn't argue with it, but people had been saying "you're next up here", so I went and warmed up, but it was Paddy who came on.

'That was the message to me: you're going to be the bit-part player if even that.

'I didn't consider leaving the panel whatsoever. I never considered that, even when I was told to go off by people. Colm O'Neill asked me on our team holiday in Mauritius would I do it again, and I said absolutely.

'You talk to Stevie, you talk to Oisín, they were gearing up for games, we were gearing up for training sessions, and that's all it was.

'It's not the same when you're not playing, that's the simple fact.'

The Ulster final against Donegal was a significant step up in quality. Mickey Moran's side were in their first provincial decider since 1998, when they were denied by a kiss-blowing Joe Brolly at the death.

The Tír Chonaill County had gained revenge in the 2002 semi-final, a match played out in farcical circumstances. The match in Clones was scheduled for a 2.40pm throw-in, two hours and ten minutes after Ireland kicked off their World Cup knockout clash with Spain.

RTÉ's attempts to have the game moved to Saturday evening were rebuffed by the Ulster Council. The late Danny Murphy, the main man in the provincial body, said that 'We feel it will still be possible for people to see the game on TV in the Clones area before making their way to the pitch in plenty of time for the start of the match.'

Even if the game in South Korea had been decided after 90 minutes, it would have been a tight rush, but Mick McCarthy's side went to extra-time and penalties before losing out.

The end result was an Ulster final expected to draw over 20,000 having a McKenna Cup attendance for the first half and not much better for the second period, with 7,394 eventually coming through the gate.

'Obviously it didn't put the players up or down, as we were preparing for a game,' says Kevin Cassidy. 'But I do remember the buzz outside the ground. Even as we went to warm up, fans were shouting to us with updates from the Ireland game.'

Armagh were back in the Ulster final for the third time in four years, and the majority of the panel already had two provincial medals in their back pocket. They knew how to win these games.

Donegal, by contrast, were lacking such experience. Jim McGuinness had been part of the 1992 Ulster and All-Ireland-winning panel. John Gildea, then 20, had helped out in training matches for that famous Tír Chonaill team ten years previously, although he wasn't officially part of the panel.

There appeared to be something different about them in 2002 though. Donegal had been labelled as the party boys in the GAA, but Moran and former Armagh coach John Morrison were attempting to cultivate a new, serious approach.

The 'shared responsibility' motto had been shaken a week before the Derry game. Brendan Devenney flew to America to play for Donegal New York when club games had been suspended back in the homeland in preparation for the northwest derby.

The prodigious Devenney, who had scored 0-14 for St Eunan's in the 1999 county final, had turned down decent money from Finn Harps to play for his county that season, and his American commitments were part of the deal.

He kept his place against Derry and, despite only getting a point off Sean Marty Lockhart, he won the crucial penalty that Adrian Sweeney converted. His place was under threat for the Armagh game though, but for far more serious reasons – a car accident.

'I was in a van that flipped into a field. It takes a lot to scare me, but it shook me up more than I probably realised. I had two cracked ribs, which I didn't tell anyone about at the time – not that Armagh would have taken advantage of that!'

He made it to Clones though, and with some new blood adding much-needed steel to the panel, Donegal entered the game in good stead.

'Donegal had a decent run in the Qualifiers in 2001 and then Mickey Moran brought myself, Rory Kavanagh and Tony McFadden in from the U21s,' says Cassidy.

'We had no baggage coming in as young lads and we didn't hold any fear of Armagh, but I suppose the older lads who had been there a while would have been a bit fragile and maybe lacked that self-belief.

'Armagh were extremely well organised and obviously massively into their strength and conditioning at that time. They did match-ups, dropping men back, whereas we just played man-on-man, and they made us pay for that.

'In that final, I went down for a ball and John Toal came in and caught me with a knee to the head. At half-time, I had no idea where I was, but I finished the game out and ended up in hospital after. There were no concussion protocols in those days, but that was Armagh at that time – totally ruthless in everything they did.'

Donegal were on the back foot from the first minute, following the concession of an unusual goal. Diarmaid Marsden, struggling to find top stride in that season's Championship, collected the ball close to the sideline and had a pop at goal. His ambitious effort dropped well short, but the slippy surface saw it bounce higher than expected.

Tír Chonaill goalkeeper Tony Blake was as surprised as anyone by the ball's trajectory. With the assistance of the crossbar, he could only palm it back out to where the onrushing John McEntee was on hand to slap home.

Mickey Moran's side were competing even after that setback, but eight first-half wides, some inexcusable, chipped away at their confidence bit by bit, even though they weren't facing an Armagh side at their fluid best.

Enda McNulty, despite picking up a hamstring injury in the opening minutes, excelled on Devenney. John McEntee nabbed 1-1 from play, and young Ronan Clarke had a superb second period, but others were struggling to get into their groove.

What did shine through was their experience, as demonstrated when Donegal's Jim McGuinness rattled the net ten minutes from time to leave it 1-11 to 1-9 in Armagh's favour. Orchard teams of the past would have crumbled, but Kernan's men scored three of the final four points.

For the last of those, Kieran McGeeney snagged a loose ball in defence and broke out from the back, before sending Eamon Doherty to The Paragon for a pint with a hand-pass dummy. Geezer went forward and tried to pick out Clarke. Although the pass carried too much steam, the forward produced a beautifully deft touch on the deck to nutmeg Raymond Sweeney, before picking the ball up and feeding Stevie McDonnell, who clipped over the clincher.

It was a rare piece of genius on a day when Armagh provided very little, but they had enough muscle memory to find a way to win. For the second time in three years, the Ulster Championship had ended with McGeeney lifting the Anglo Celt Cup above his head.

In 2000, he was visibly beaming when presented with the trophy on the pitch. Two years on, now on the steps of the Gerry Arthurs Stand and with his manager in tears below him, McGeeney wore a contented smile. There was clearly only one trophy that would sate his hunger.

Afterwards, with a fan in an Ian Paisley mask attempting to distract him, Geezer told the waiting press that 'the job isn't done yet'. John McEntee called the win 'a stepping stone'.

'We know we are good enough to beat anyone,' Joe Kernan concluded.

That 'anyone' included Tyrone, but a third meeting with the Red Hands would have been unpalatable. An uneasiness had accompanied Armagh's march to the Ulster title in 2002. A small seed of doubt had become rooted in the back of players' minds, and was even more prominent in those of their supporters. Tyrone.

A sense of inevitability hung about the championship that year.

Armagh and Tyrone would cross paths again and the deck would be stacked in the favour of the Red Hands. The message in the Tyrone dressing room after their loss to Armagh earlier in the season was a simple one: 'We'll get those bastards later in the year, and this time we'll make them pay.'

The motivation would be theirs and Peter Canavan was already back to full fitness, leading Derry on a merry dance in the Qualifiers. What's more, the rivals could only meet from the semi-final onwards, so if it did come around the stakes would be huge.

That game was starting to come into view early on in Tyrone's Qualifier clash with Sligo at Croke Park. Art McRory and Eugene McKenna's men were justifying their tag as favourites and raced into a 0-8 to 0-2 lead.

Canavan nabbed two early points, while Declan McCrossan and Brian McGuigan were racking up the assists. The overrun Connacht outfit had Eamonn O'Hara offering almost sole resistance. Peter the Great was at his mesmerising best, breaking the ankles of Patrick Naughton with a series of feints and checks every time the ball went forward in those opening 20 minutes.

The Armagh players would have been watching, and watching with worry – unnecessarily, as it turned out.

The term 'negative spiral' exists in sporting psychology, and largely concerns momentum shifts. At Croke Park on that warm July day, something happened to change the energy of the game, and Tyrone simply couldn't stop it.

There was no big moment, such as a Sligo goal, but in a negative spiral, athletes overthink simple mistakes and their reaction is to try harder. Trying too hard invariably leads to more mistakes, and the spiral continues downward.

In the wide open spaces of Croke Park, a mostly youthful Tyrone demon-strated in front of the watching public that they lacked the experience to win an All-Ireland title in 2002. When Canavan tapped over a close-in free in the 24th minute, Tyrone led 0-9 to 0-3, but they wouldn't score again in the first half, while Sligo tagged on four scores.

Mistakes were creeping in. Naughton, begging for mercy from Canavan, moved onto Stevie O'Neill and twice blocked him down. Brian McGuigan was coughing up easy possession, something he didn't do in the first quar-ter. In defence, Conor Gormley and Cormac McGinley were steaming into tackles and giving away cheap frees.

Tyrone had lost their way. The half-time whistle was warmly received by the Ulster side as they departed the Croke Park pitch with a two-point advantage.

The negative spiral appeared to have been arrested when the game restarted, with Tyrone hitting three of the first four points to lead 0-12 to 0-8 after 42 minutes. Incredibly, and once again bringing their inexperi-ence to the surface, they would fail to score from there.

The cue for the momentum shift was more obvious in this half. In the 44th minute, Eamon O'Hara picked up the ball and, from 45 metres out, launched a massive score that just made it over Peter Ward's bar. The Sligo crowd – and the fans from Donegal and Meath coming in for their game afterwards – responded, with O'Hara gesturing for his team and the crowd to ratchet it up. The introduction of Paul Taylor, a real fan favourite, also cranked up the atmosphere.

It worked. Sligo would score 1-5 without reply, to complete a remarkable turnaround. Tyrone were out, and all in the Orchard County – players, fans and management – breathed a collective sigh of relief. In his *Irish Examiner* column, former Galway All-Ireland captain Ray Silke described Tyrone as an Armadillo – 'hard on the outside and soft on the inside'.

The draw for the All-Ireland quarter-finals was staged on 'The Sunday Game' the following weekend. Armagh couldn't draw Donegal, so it was Kerry, Mayo or Sligo for Joe Kernan's side. Either Connacht county would have been welcomed, but when Sligo came out, it presented two great opportunities.

Firstly, it was a very favourable path back to the semi-final. Secondly, it was a perfect opportunity to bury Armagh's Croke Park hoodoo.

The Ulster side's inability to win at Headquarters had become a regular media focus when analysing their visits to the famous venue. Inside the dressing room it carried little weight, but there was a compelling case that Armagh choked when they got there.

Joe Kernan didn't buy into any talk of curses. He had won at Croke Park as Armagh defeated Roscommon in the 1977 All-Ireland semi-final.

The problem was that the county hadn't won a championship game there since.

There was the '77 final loss to Dublin; semi-final defeats to Roscommon, Kerry and Meath in 1980, '82 and '99; a semi-final draw and replay loss to Kerry in 2000; and the sliding doors 2001 Qualifier exit at the hands of Galway.

This time, though, they couldn't have picked a better draw to end that run. A few weeks earlier in Clontibret, Sligo had edged a challenge match between the sides, but putting stock in challenge match results is an exercise in futility.

Clearly the Yeatsmen were no mugs – victory over Tyrone had served notice of that – but Ray Silke's pre-match description of Armagh suggested the Orchard were 'a big Sherman tank grinding their opponents to pulp'. Sligo would surely be bulldozed out of their path.

For 25 minutes, that tank rolled over anything in black and white. Armagh led 1-5 to 0-3 and were playing some scintillating football, with Stevie McDonnell stroking home an early goal. Diarmaid Marsden's composed finish put them six points up early in the second half and when John McEntee quickly tagged on a point, the tank was on cruise control.

When Sligo's David Durkin was sent off for foolishly swiping at McDonnell, it should have been curtains for the Connacht side. Any team with serious ambitions of All-Ireland glory would have extinguished any lingering threat there and then.

Instead, Sligo, just as they had against Tyrone, came on strong. With Armagh not scoring in the final 20 minutes and the Yeats County grabbing four points in a row, the gap was cut to the minimum with minutes remaining.

Then a mistake in the Armagh backline sent Dara McGarty through. One on one, he had two options – fist over and settle for the draw, or go for broke and accept the role of hero or villain dictated by the outcome.

McGarty took the safe option and, on reflection, it was one of the biggest moments of Armagh's season. When the player got married in 2017, his best man played a video message from Benny Tierney thanking him for the role he played in Armagh's All-Ireland success.

The Armagh players were locked in the dressing room for 30 minutes after the game and torn to shreds. It was a display lacking authority, one that severely dented any perception that Sam Maguire was coming.

One player feeling relief rather than disappointment was Justin McNulty. His blocked-down shot had led to Galway's winner in 2001, and his misplaced pass had allowed McGarty in.

It was a chastening day for management too. Armagh's route-one approach paid early dividends, but when Sligo found a way around it, Kernan's side looked rudderless. The filtering back of players in the final quarter, described by the Sligo Champion as 'paranoid cynicism', to try to see out the game was negativity personified. Kernan's claim that he couldn't get the message across to Barry O'Hagan to move forward because of crowd noise was a feeble enough excuse.

By the time the team arrived back at the Carrickdale Hotel on the border, Kernan had found the authoritative voice that seemed to have abandoned all involved a few hours earlier. The message was direct – Armagh are still in the All-Ireland Championship.

The one previous Championship meeting between Armagh and Sligo had been in 1926 in the Junior Championship, and it had also required a replay. Jim Kernan, uncle of Joe, was one of the scorers as Armagh won the replay in Cavan.

Against the Breffni County three years later, Jim Kernan would be involved in a collision with Jim Smith that would lead to his death a couple of days later. The cause of death was peritonitis following perforation, a hole in the intestine causing serious complications.

The Cavan captain was arrested and it was attested that 'on Sunday, June 30 at Belturbet he did feloniously kill and slay one James Kernan of Crossmaglen, Co Armagh'.

GAA President Seán Ryan defended the Cavan player and, with a stream of witnesses testifying that the clash was accidental, Smith was cleared. He would go on to become the first Ulster man to lift the Sam Maguire, in 1933.

Ten Ulster players had since followed his lead, in 11 Sam Maguire triumphs – Cavan's John Joe O'Reilly having the honour of lifting the famous trophy twice – but none of those had worn orange and white, and Sligo were intent on keeping it that way.

Páirc Tailteann in Navan was the chosen venue for the replay rather than a return to Croke Park. Sligo had protested the original decision of Clones, given that the Monaghan venue had essentially become Armagh's home from home.

Kernan felt that some fans would miss out as a result, but privately he would have been relieved for the hoodoo to fade out into the background. Kernan liked the venue too, if not the weather he had experienced there. His last visit as manager had been in February 1999, when Crossmaglen had defeated Carlow's Éire Óg in an All-Ireland semi-final in absolutely atrocious conditions.

Sligo and drama went hand-in-hand in 2002, and there was plenty of it on offer in Navan again. Another seven-point comeback, a controversial penalty claim turned down and a Garda escort for referee Seamus McCormack. Full-time: Armagh 1-16 Sligo 0-17.

'That day in Navan, how we got out of there without the referee giving that penalty,' says former Orchard joint-manager Brian Canavan. 'Joe carried with him that bit of luck that we maybe didn't have. I'm friendly with a few guys from Sligo, and to this day they still talk about it.'

The match followed the same pattern as the first. Armagh once again led by two points at the interval. They once again hit the net early in the second half, Ronan Clarke displaying fabulous footwork to fool the opposition before slotting home.

Like the first game, Sligo were wounded, but as long as they had breath in their bodies, they were going to fight. Back they came, point by point, and once again Sligo were presented with a match-winning opportunity at the death.

Dara McGarty broke through the cover and fisted across to the onrushing Sean Davey. With the goal in his sight, it looked like substitute Tony McEntee tugged the jersey of Davey before a stream of orange bodies crowded him out.

In real time it looked a penalty, but a slowed-down replay showed that, while McEntee's hand was on Davey's shoulder, he was not tugging or pushing. Given that referees do not have the luxury of a second look, Armagh could count themselves lucky the whistle didn't sound.

Those moments had gone against them in the years before. Maybe Joe Kernan was a lucky general. Maybe the tide was turning. All that mattered was that Armagh were in the All-Ireland semi-final. Dublin were waiting.

Chapter Nine

Conquering the Hill

G iven the pressures of securing tickets for Armagh games in 2002, those helter-skelter affairs on the pitch were wee buns. By the time Dublin came into view, the scramble was at fever pitch.

The mood was tense in the Dromintee clubhouse days before that semi-final. Everyone knew the drill at this stage, given how many big games Armagh had been involved in in recent years. With the evening turning from dusk to dark at the foot of Slieve Gullion, members piled into the hall and took their seats, awaiting their own lotto.

Demand would always outweigh supply, leading to an old-fashioned draw from a hat. Armagh had received around 20,000 tickets, with their opponents being allocated 22,000. Croke Park manager Peter McKenna estimated that they could have sold 120,000 for the match, with Longford also searching for a big allocation for their minor semi-final meeting with Derry, who traditionally didn't bring a huge following.

This was not a normal ticket draw though. The GAA had intervened after pressure from Armagh, and approval from the Gardaí, and had taken the unusual step of giving the Ulster side 2,000 tickets for Hill 16, breaking up the traditional sky blue that usually dominates the famed terrace.

Armagh's hustle for those Hill tickets was twofold. For one, Hill 16 tickets were to cost €15, as against €35 for the stands. Secondly, and of utmost importance in the psychological warfare, orange on the Hill would be a statement. Orange men on the march over Dublin land.

In Dromintee, as the nervous patrons awaited the draw, MC for the night Declan Fearon made an announcement: 'We have been given a couple of Hill 16 tickets, if anyone is brave enough to take them.' A group of teenagers who had followed Armagh everywhere, looked at each other, shrugged their shoulders and made their way forward. No draw needed.

'Collect your crash helmets too,' Fearon added, to much laughter.

When the pre-match parade moved in front of the Hill, two large patches of orange were present on the terrace. The Gardaí were nervous about the situation and when Armagh fans entered through the turnstiles, they were told to stay away from the Nally side.

As orange-and-white banners were unfurled, Orchard fans had to endure a few taunts about occupied land up in the north of the country. Yet here they were, marching on sacred ground.

It all added to what was one of the great Croke Park atmospheres. Typically, both counties had sourced many tickets above their allocation and, with the weather glorious and a recently renovated Croke Park looking resplendent, all the ingredients were there for a classic.

There was also something else on the line – the apparently inevitable renewal of the game's most famous rivalry.

The week before, Kerry had decimated Munster rivals Cork in the first semi-final. With Tommy Lyons's Dublin side meanwhile building momentum at every juncture, another chapter was to be written. Dublin and Kerry had met 22 times prior to that in the Championship, with exactly half of those encounters being in All-Ireland finals.

Throw in a new darling of the Hill and the pieces were all falling into place.

Ray Cosgrove was leading the charge of the capital's new gun-slingers. He had hit the net twice to earn Dublin's first win over Meath since 1995, and another green flag had secured the Leinster title at the expense of Kildare.

The two-game saga with Donegal had produced three more goals – six in all ahead of Armagh. Four had been into the Hill, with kisses to the crowd and manic celebrations. Cossie was one of the star stories of the 2002 season and his six majors were more than Dublin as a whole had managed in five of the six seasons since their last Sam Maguire triumph in 1995.

Add Ciaran Whelan's barnstorming runs from the middle, the emergence of carefree youngster Alan Brogan and fan favourite Jason Sherlock's cameos from the bench, and it was an electrifying tonic of positivity and possibilities.

Not all in blue were enjoying drinking that dizzying concoction. Speaking to the *Irish Independent* before the Armagh game, Dublin captain

Coman Goggins was clearly disturbed by the seemingly pre-ordained outcome.

'The press are talking about a Dublin and Kerry final. I'm telling you, it's right up their street. It's just all Dublin, Dublin, Dublin. You'd wonder are you being set up for a big shock here.'

Tommy Lyons uttered similar sentiments to the RTÉ cameras. He felt that some of his players had bought into the hype, and said that he would have loved to be in Joe Kernan's shoes.

His opposite number wasn't short on scrutiny either. Once again, much of the focus was on the county's love/hate relationship with Croke Park – they seemed to hate it, while their opponents loved playing them there.

Minutes before throw-in, Pat Spillane in the 'Sunday Game' studio was taking aim.

'This crowd have been here for several years,' he said of the Ulster champions. 'They're well experienced, they're around a long time. At the back of their minds, it's '77 since they won their last championship match [at Croke Park].

'This is one of the things – you talk about the hype with the Dubs, but you also have a mental block, a mental problem, a psychological thing with Armagh, because there is this so-called Croke Park hoodoo.'

Spillane and fellow pundit Colm O'Rourke plumped for a Dublin victory. The Meath man suggested that Diarmaid Marsden, who adorned the match programme cover, was the embodiment of Armagh – a player who starts like a train, but has run out of confidence and slows as the final destination appears.

The sidelines were feeling the tension and, as the teams took part in the pre-match parade amid a blare of noise from all around the ground, the players would have been feeling it too. They had never experienced noise like it.

Stevie McDonnell said that the blast of orange infiltrating the sea of blue was noticed.

'The orange and white in the stadiums back then was unreal. You're on the pitch, focussed, but you are taking it in, and you see this wave of colour on the Hill and it's just beautiful.

'I always said after that match that Dublin were my new second team. There was a guy living beside me in Killeavy from Dublin – he still lives there – and his dad was always a steward at Croke Park when we were playing all those big games there. In the pre-match parades he'd be calling to me, so I always did enjoy the Dublin support.

'I've always said this, and I've yet to do it, but I would love to go to the Hill for a Dublin match. I've never been in the Hill in my life for a game. I've been there for promotional events and photos, but I've never watched a game on Hill 16, and it's something I will do.'

The parade started at 3.24pm, six minutes after Armagh had left the dressing room, and those final moments were the most torturous for Kieran McGeeney. The opening shot of the war was moments away and these duties were delaying combat. As the Artane Band turned the corner from Hill 16 to the Cusack Stand side, Geezer nearly trampled over the flag bearer in front of him, a ball of pent-up energy.

He needed to save it though. The calendar may have flipped from August to September some fifteen and a half hours earlier, but the temperature at Croke Park was over 20 degrees at throw-in. La Manga weather.

Half of the Armagh defence, McGeeney included, were very familiar with the opposition, as they played their club football in the capital.

McGeeney was with Na Fianna, and would be coming up against club-mates Senan Connell, Dessie Farrell and Jason Sherlock. Ballyboden had four players on show at Croke Park. Enda McNulty and Andrew McCann started for Armagh, while Darren Homan and Colin Moran came off the bench for the Dubs.

McGeeney kept his troops in the huddle for an eternity, one finger raised as final instructions were relayed.

The Armagh–Dublin semi-final of 2002 is regarded as a classic encounter but, in reality, it was a game with one absolutely brilliant half and one half of pure averageness.

Just four seconds had elapsed when Geezer lined Ciaran Whelan up for a shoulder, but his timing was a split-second out and the Dublin midfielder was able to maintain his balance. The Armagh captain was pumped.

Tommy Lyons would have been delighted by his side's start. Senan Connell opened the scoring and then Ray Cosgrove grabbed an important score.

The Kilmacud man may have run riot all summer, but Armagh were very confident of bullying him into his shell. In the sixth minute, he collected the ball close to the Canal End goal and was immediately sandwiched by Francie Bellew, Kieran McGeeney and Enda McNulty. All three bounced off the Dublin man and he doubled his side's advantage.

When Darren Magee took a Benny Tierney kick-out, raced through and split the posts, Armagh's hate affair with the Jones' Road venue looked destined to continue.

Relief and respite arrived via a Paddy McKeever free – his first score since the Ulster semi-final against Fermanagh – and a stunning effort from McDonnell.

Armagh defender Andy Mallon tracks Gary Kavanagh of Laois in the 2003 All-Ireland quarter-final at Croke Park.

Above: Armagh forward Martin O'Rourke attempts to get past Tyrone pair Philip Jordan (left) and Michael McGee (right) in their 2003 National League meeting in Omagh.

Below: Dublin goalkeeper Stephen Cluxton is sent off just minutes after Paddy McKeever had been lined in the 2003 All-Ireland Qualifier between Armagh and Dublin at Croke Park.

The highly controversial clash between Armagh's Diarmaid Marsden and Tyrone's Philip Jordan in the 2003 All-Ireland final. The Armagh player was sent off.

Above: Eamon Maguire, Fermanagh, is tackled by Armagh's (left to right) Philip Loughran, Kieran Hughes, Aidan O'Rourke, and Andy Mallon during the 2004 All-Ireland quarter-final at Croke Park.

Below: Armagh and Tyrone players clash during the 2005 Ulster final replay at Croke Park.

Armagh captain Kieran McGeeney is substituted towards the end of the county's 2005 All-Ireland semi-final loss to Tyrone.

Armagh defender Ciaran McKeever after Tyrone were awarded the winning free at the end of the 2005 All-Ireland semi-final at Croke Park.

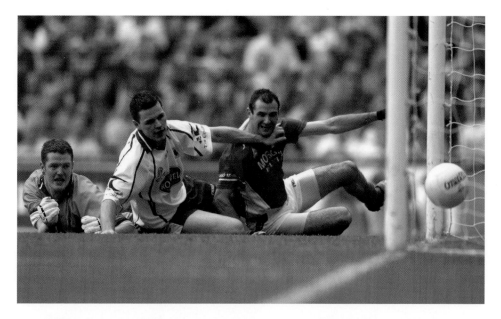

Above: Tyrone goalkeeper Pascal McConnell and defender Conor Gormley watch on as Armagh's Stevie McDonnell hits the net from a near-impossible angle in the 2005 All-Ireland semi-final at Croke Park.

Below: Kerry full-forward Kieran Donaghy roars in the face of Armagh goalkeeper Paul Hearty during the 2006 All-Ireland quarter-final.

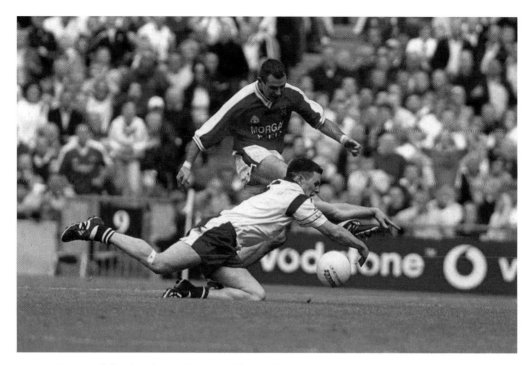

Tyrone defender Conor Gormley blocks down Armagh's Stevie McDonnell, preventing the Orchard County from getting a levelling goal late on in the 2005 All-Ireland semi-final.

Armagh's shooting was generally poor though. John McEntee, twice, Diarmaid Marsden and Oisín McConville kicked bad wides while McConville also mis-hit a '45', although Stephen Cluxton had to be alert to stop McDonnell from flicking it to the net.

The contest wasn't helped by fussy officiating from Michael Collins. Armagh were undoubtedly the beneficiaries in the first half, as Dublin were cited for a series of minor misdemeanours. The Hill told him as much in the 18th minute, with a chant that wasn't suitable for daytime TV.

That was also the minute when McConville levelled things up. Ray Cosgrove, despite loud, unsporting boos from the Armagh fans, edged Dublin ahead again going into the second quarter.

Crucially, Paul McGrane and John Toal were starting to get control around the middle, having struggled, especially under their own kick-outs, in the opening stages. By the time of the semi-final, McGrane, Ciaran Whelan and Darragh Ó Sé were considered the three best midfielders in the country, but Armagh's central pairing came as a package.

When Toal rocked up for his first Armagh training session after being called in by Brian McAlinden and Brian Canavan, the first person to come over and welcome him was McGrane. Their relationship developed from there and now they were backing each other up in the heat of an All-Ireland semi-final.

Toal had joined the panel as a tall but slight player, and was deployed as a half-forward in the early days. McAlinden in particular came down hard on him to toughen him up. 'Brian was very good and he was very honest. Whether you liked it or not, he told you what he thought – something he did with me on a few occasions.

'That could have been good or bad, but you took it whatever way you wanted. He'd tell me that my physique wasn't what it needed to be, or maybe I needed to work on this angle of my game. But he'd tell me when I'm doing something well. They were very honest as a management team; they were straight with you and you respected that.'

Those improvements were evident in a half where Armagh failed to find real rhythm. Their attackers were fluffing their lines, with half a dozen first-half wides in all – a shot accuracy of 43 per cent. Oisín McConville was short with a '45' and Diarmaid Marsden hit the post, but Toal and McGrane were now ensuring that there was a steady stream of possession coming their way.

Ronan Clarke kicked a fine score in a move started by Enda McNulty, who was giving Alan Brogan a lesson, but Dublin responded quickly. Cosgrove was once again the scoring source, with a point from play and another from a free.

Armagh were level by the break though, with McConville chipping over a generously awarded free and a second on the whistle that was as nailed on as they come.

When Michael Collins blew his half-time whistle, he was once again serenaded unfavourably by the Hill as the teams trekked off, having shared 12 points. Armagh's assistant manager Paul Grimley was nabbed for a few words by RTÉ's Darragh Maloney en route to the dressing room. While steam wasn't escaping his ears, Grimley didn't look overly pleased with what he had witnessed.

'If you found that breath-taking, then you're suffering from acute bron-chitis,' Pat Spillane offered up.

The Go Games mini-sevens would provide entertainment at the break. Future county players such as Armagh's Anto Duffy, Cavan's Gearoid McKiernan, Derry's Emmet McGuckin, Fermanagh's Chris O'Brien and

Down's Keith Quinn featured, while Armagh and Dublin plotted ahead for one of the most important 35 minutes of any of their lives.

It was now, at the interval, that the seeds of Joe Kernan's legend really started to take root.

A football jersey was a special thing to the Orchard manager. Something earned through blood, sweat and tears. A cherished memento. Even though Kernan and his team-mates lost out in the 1977 All-Ireland final against Dublin, his jersey from that day was very close to his heart.

Now, in the bowels of Croke Park, that jersey – long sleeved and completely orange, apart from a white collar and the number eight on the back – was held aloft in front of the 2002 squad and the question was asked, 'How much do you want an All-Ireland final jersey of your own?'

'I remember when I was playing, when we played Dublin, we were hammered. Brian Mullins is a good friend and he asked me, did I want to swap jerseys? I said, "I'll take yours, but you're not getting mine,"' Kernan says.

'To me, my jersey was too important. I earned the right to wear it and I wasn't going to give it to someone else. I see it like a Western – I'm not going to give my scalp to fucking someone else. I didn't want boys training in Derry or Dublin with my scalp on them.

'To me, my jersey should have been given to a sick child in a hospital, or a family friend or a child or relative. Let them appreciate the jersey.

'I never thought I would be using a jersey 25 years later in an All-Ireland semi-final, telling everyone that I wanted them to have what I had. It's amazing that wee things are so important. You have to have pride. Wearing it is not enough; you don't throw it on the ground or give it away.'

Armagh lifted the intensity immediately as the second period began, none more so than half-backs Aidan O'Rourke and Andrew McCann, who were instantly looking busier. Three minutes into the second half, the latter forced a great turnover on Senan Connell. John Toal picked up the scraps and kicked towards Stevie McDonnell, who turned on a sixpence and launched a missile between the posts to put Armagh ahead for the first time.

Moments later, Connell, after good link-up play with Ray Cogsrove, who was still getting change out of Francie Bellew, pointed another fine effort. Already the second half was starting to look like the gladiatorial battle that spectators inside the Croke Park Colosseum were demanding.

Then came the most exciting minute of the 2002 Championship season.

Paul McGrane, who was now completely ruling the roost in midfield, took a fine catch off a Stephen Cluxton kick-out and left two opponents in his wake. He played the ball to Stevie McDonnell, who recycled it back out to John Toal.

French writer Claude-Frédéric Bastiat once said that 'repetition may not entertain, but it teaches'. In this moment, Armagh's telepathy, developed over years in the trenches, paid rich dividends.

Toal was 45 metres out and with a slight breeze in his favour, just inside shooting range. But when he drew his foot back, Paddy McKeever knew exactly where the ball was going – to Diarmaid Marsden on the edge of the square. A split second after Toal connected, McKeever was making a beeline for the square.

Dublin defender Barry Cahill managed to break the ball away from Marsden's grasp, but McKeever was ready to pounce.

Picking up possession, a clever side-step took Stephen Cluxton out of the equation. As McKeever attempted to shoot to an empty net, he was bear-hugged by Paddy Christie. The ball rolled over the line after the player got the faintest of touches.

Referee Michael Collins looked slightly unsure, but his umpire immediately raised the green flag and McKeever's confident celebration put any doubt out of his mind.

'You know your players after a while and I knew that there was a ball coming from John,' said McKeever. 'He launched one in. Diarmaid was always good in that if he wasn't able to get the ball, he at least would do enough to make sure you had a chance of getting something off him.

'It was about taking that chance with the run. I don't know how clear it was to those watching, but I made an inclination to shoot and Stephen Cluxton bought it. That let me skip around him, and then I was tackled around the waist, but I made contact.'

There was 40:15 on the clock when McKeever put Armagh 1-7 to 0-7 ahead. It took just 48 seconds for Dublin to level the scores once again.

A quick Cluxton kick-out found Johnny Magee. He passed to Dessie Farrell, who was crudely fouled by his clubmate and marker for the day Kieran McGeeney. It was one of the rare moments when McGeeney was switched off. Seconds later, Enda McNulty also tuned out as he allowed Alan Brogan to steal a march.

Brogan collected Farrell's free kick and offloaded to the onrushing Ciaran Whelan, who rampaged through the middle like a force of nature.

Armagh's concentration had been knocked by the giddiness of their own goal and their minds were temporarily fogged by the noise that greeted McKeever's strike.

Aidan O'Rourke was the exception. Spotting exactly what was going on as Whelan surged forward, he made a gallant, yet futile, sprint from his position on the left to try to block the shot. The ball just escaped his fingers, arced over Benny Tierney, kissed the underside of the crossbar and rested in the Hill 16 net.

O'Rourke wasn't generally given to emotion on the field, but he lay prone on the ground for a number of seconds, staring at the size-five O'Neills resting in the goal. In the blink of an eye, Armagh had turned positive momentum into negative. The doubts developed by years of near misses were jostling for position in Orchard hearts and minds.

'Forget the first half; this is the second half,' commentator Marty Morrissey told the watching public.

When Brogan kicked over with his left to regain the lead for the Dubs, Armagh's dreams were starting to fracture. The pressure wasn't confined to the Ulster side though. Cosgrove, who had given Bellew a tough day, spilled a routine ball that surely would have led to another point. O'Rourke stepped in to collect possession and passed it out to Toal, who kicked it forward to John McEntee. The Crossmaglen man ran down a blind alley, but was given time to correct himself, turn onto his left and level things up.

The game swung back Dublin's way over the next couple of plays. Collie Moran, given too much space by Justin McNulty, put them back in front before Whelan went on another rampage forward, meeting John McEntee's shoulder and sending the Armagh man back a yard – no easy feat – with his shot just clearing the crossbar.

McKeever, dropped for the replay win over Sligo, kept Armagh in touch while Whelan was starting to undo some of his good work by getting agitated by John Toal. He gave away two frees in quick succession, and picked up a yellow card for throwing the ball at the Keady man's head. John McEntee levelled the scores for the seventh time after the second of those frees was worked forward.

As the hour mark approached, Dublin were two in front again. Alan Brogan, a below-par first half shed from his memory, pointed confidently before Cosgrove added another decent score.

Armagh were doing exactly what Armagh were expected to do – finding a way to lose a match at Croke Park when the game was in the balance. Even their own fans were losing faith. Armagh's reputation as chokers looked set to be copper-fastened.

The tag would finally be shattered forever in the final 15-odd minutes of the contest. Of the five remaining scores in the game, four would come from Joe Kernan's men.

Prominent in that final charge was Oisín McConville, who had been on the periphery until this point. The Crossmaglen legend has a reputation for speaking his mind no matter what the situation, and there are few instances when he regrets the words that have come out of his mouth.

One comment does stand out though, and this was his portrayal of Dublin defender Paul Casey in his book. Describing him as 'not great', McConville said that he had effectively been handed a free pass by Tommy Lyons's decision to put the Lucan man on him.

'I met Paul after; that wasn't the way it was meant to be in the book, him being an easy touch. That was wrong,' McConville says. 'I just felt that I could get the better of him. It sounds demeaning that I would say that about another guy going out to play for his county. Paul Casey was not a bad footballer, but I knew on the way into that game that I was going to have opportunities and I'd have a decent game.

'I didn't have the game of my life or anything, but I had a decent day. I had a lot of possession; could have had two more scores in the first half that I kicked wide.'

McConville converted a free off the deck to halve the deficit, but Cosgrove would escape Bellew's clutches for one last time to kick Dublin's final score – his fourth point from play. Any thoughts that he could be bullied out of it had been emphatically answered. Seconds later, Jason Sherlock was introduced, to a deafening roar from the Hill.

The foundations for Sky Blue joy were being laid, but 19-year-old Ronan Clarke shook them with a sky-scraper, before Darren Homan tested their sturdiness further, butchering what should have been a routine point by dropping it into Benny Tierney's hands. Armagh quickly worked it forward, where the impressive John McEntee stroked casually over. All square, five minutes left.

Next, McGeeney broke forward and directed a left-footed effort towards McConville. It wasn't the most accurate of passes and the player had to fight in the air to fend off Casey, but the moment he took control of the ball, his ruthless instincts kicked in. He was going for the kill.

Most players would have turned and recycled possession out towards a waiting half-forward, but McConville put the head down, breezed past Casey along the end-line and fisted over. Armagh's clutch player had just grabbed his first point from play, and it would turn out to be the winner.

Having spent 69 minutes giving Armagh the rub of the green, Michael Collins went full circle from there on in.

First John McEntee was cited, despite a brilliant dispossession that would have left Armagh on the counter in a dangerous part of the pitch. Then Kieran McGeeney didn't win a free after shipping a high shoulder from Jason Sherlock. When the ball broke, Francie Bellew's brute strength saw him overpower the Dublin man, but Collins pointed towards the Hill.

That was wasted after Aidan O'Rourke, heroic in the second half, held up Alan Brogan, but Dublin would get one last, dramatic, controversial chance.

Chants of 'Armagh, Armagh' were reverberating around the newly refurbished stadium when Marty Morrisey asked, 'Is the dream final about to be interrupted?'

Two minutes of additional time had been indicated. One minute and 50 seconds of this had elapsed when Michael Collins penalised Enda McNulty for a foul on Ray Cosgrove. Soft as they come.

The kick was just outside of routine range, but inside the expected zone.

Cosgrove took two deep breaths, and five steps forward took him in a central channel. The ball was kicked hard and high, a right-to-left curl taking it back towards its destination. But space ran out and the shot hit the post and rebounded back into play.

Six players reacted in the fight for possession; five of those were wearing orange. Justin McNulty rose above Dessie Farrell and flicked the ball towards Francie Bellew. The Crossmaglen man fumbled possession, but had time to put his toe under it, pick it up and fist to teammate John McEntee just as the referee brought proceedings to an end.

Cosgrove had lit up the All-Ireland series, but history is written by the victors. His most memorable contribution would be that missed free at the death – a reminder of the never-ending cruelty of the sporting arena. Cosgrove deserved a different ending to his summer of scintillation.

Aidan O'Rourke and John McEntee embraced and hopped up the pitch, a frustrated Jason Sherlock kicking out at them petulantly as they passed. Joe Kernan commiserated and Tommy Lyons congratulated. While the Orchard County's traditional pitch invasion didn't come to pass, a few stragglers did manage to evade the stewards.

'My wife Patricia always says the Dublin game was better than the final,' says Joe Kernan. 'After three years, people thought we were doomed and cursed; a load of shite. It was always about what we would do. You never go looking for an excuse. Either we did it or we didn't, it's as simple as that.

'When the free kick was being taken, I told Paul McGrane to stay in Ray Cosgrove's eye-line. If you watch the video, Paul ran alongside it.

'Who got the rebound only Francie. Francie gave it to John Mac. There was a "buck-lep" over at the sideline and all hell broke loose.'

Pockets of orange erupted around the ground. The 2,000 Armagh fans on Hill 16 had received a frosty reception on their arrival to that cherished ground, but Dublin fans streamed up to shake their hands and wish them well against Kerry as they started their downtrodden exit from the ground.

'My abiding memory actually comes from after the game, when we were on the bus going away from Croke Park towards home and the Dublin supporters lined the streets applauding us,' says Stevie McDonnell. 'That made us feel great – knowing you were heading into your first final and knowing you had gained respect.'

The Armagh players would join their manager in getting All-Ireland final jerseys of their own after all. The Croke Park hoodoo had been smashed into pieces. There was just one thing left to do.

Kieran McGeeney was interviewed seconds after the full-time whistle and asked for his thoughts.

'We still haven't got anything.'

One more step. There could be no going back now.

Chapter Ten

Thine is the Kingdom

One hundred years, give or take, of want. One hundred years of casting an envious eye as 16 other counties were crowned All-Ireland champions, with orange and white ribbons never adorning the Sam Maguire Cup.

A century of near misses, no hoping, no point even trying. One hundred years of living in the shadows and believing that's where you belonged. One hundred years of not being good enough and wondering would your day ever come.

One hundred years of football, during Home Rule, the War of Independence and the Troubles. One hundred years of Bill McCorry's missed penalty, Heffo's Army, the Frank McGuigan final, 'The Boys in Red and Black' and bloody Maurice Fitzgerald.

'A hundred years of suppression, of fucking helicopters, of jack-booted troops kicking them when they were down – the lot,' as the late Kerry manager Páidí Ó Sé said in his *Irish Independent* column.

And then, on 22 September 2002, neatly at the end of the 100th time that Armagh had entered the All-Ireland Championship, as historical interruptions had caused some absent years, the Orchard County stepped out of the shadows. That September Sunday, Croke Park's rafters shook as referee John Bannon brought the longest of waits to an end.

Justin McNulty, the man who had had to shoulder most of the blame for their All-Ireland exit to Galway the year before, made the final interception as he tapped the ball down to Tony McEntee. The Crossmaglen man was one of two substitutes used by manager Joe Kernan.

The other, after 17 minutes, was Barry O'Hagan, brought on after John McEntee suffered an early concussion. Like McNulty, this was O'Hagan's redemption song – he had shipped plenty of criticism for not putting the ball dead in the 2000 All-Ireland semi-final with Kerry, allowing Maurice Fitzgerald to land an equalising free. The fact he had earlier taken Éamonn Fitzmaurice for 1-1 from play from centre half-forward no longer seemed to matter.

Tony McEntee had time to deliver one last fist pass before the sound of Bannon's whistle was music to the soul of Orchardmen and women everywhere. That was to Kieran McGeeney, the man who had come to embody this Armagh team.

Almost every Armagh player celebrated in an identical fashion – two arms raised to the heavens. McGeeney was the exception – with the O'Neills ball tucked tightly in his left arm, he raised his right hand into the air before bringing it to his head in disbelief. Onto the knees then and engulfed by teammates Tony McEntee, Philip Loughran and Paddy McKeever.

Six minutes and 31 seconds after Bannon's full-time whistle, McGeeney became the first man in Armagh history to ever raise Sam Maguire as a winning captain. In their 100th attempt, Armagh became the 17th county to join the roll of honour.

And the first man the RTÉ cameras picked up trying to break onto the field was wearing a Down jersey. 'I've had slagging for that for 20 years. I thought it was over and now you're bringing it right back,' the fan in question, Derek Murphy, says with a laugh.

There are three places where the ribbing involved in the Down/Armagh rivalry is at its sharpest point – pubs, schools and building sites.

On a building site in 2002, Murphy, originally from Glenn, was arguing with some Armagh supporters about the Orchard County's 1977 run to the All-Ireland final.

'Down didn't want to see us win,' his workmates claimed.

'I supported you,' Murphy argued back.

It sparked a bit of craic about Down having five titles and Armagh zero. Murphy went to the Buttercrane Shopping Centre and bought a new Down top to wear on site.

Knowing that Murphy was heading to the final with his Armagh-mad daughter, workmate Paddy Finnegan dared him to wear the top to Croke Park. Murphy gladly accepted the challenge and headed towards the ground on the day of the final. Only when the throngs of orange tops thickened did he think a jacket might have been a good idea.

'It got worse at the stadium. I had swapped tickets so I could sit beside my daughter, and we were in amongst Camlough people,' he says.

'Our tickets were two rows from the front, so we had to walk the whole way down. There was just silence.'

As full-time approached, a cameraman approached that section of the ground to get footage of the celebrations. He stood directly in front of Murphy, who told him in an agricultural way to please move.

'He wasn't one bit pleased – he couldn't use that shot because I was going mad in it. I saw him go over and start chatting to that steward who ended up grabbing me, like everyone saw on TV. At the end of the match, my daughter went around me and flying out. I went to go after her and the steward grabbed me and pulled me back. All of this right in front of the cameraman, who must have been loving that shot.'

When Murphy pulled on his red-and-black top that morning, he didn't think that Down's five-title lead was in serious jeopardy.

Even after riding their luck against Sligo, even after edging out Dublin, Armagh's rivals would have had confidence in Kerry saving them from that phrase that they never thought they'd hear, a noise that sounded like nails on a blackboard:

'Armagh have been crowned All-Ireland champions.'

For the record, Murphy, just like he would have been in 1977, was happy to see the Orchard County get their first title.

The Kingdom were 1/2 odds on with most bookies. Warm favourites, but not overwhelmingly so.

Kerry's National League campaign was nothing special. They had lost to both Limerick and Louth, but they recovered enough to secure the Division Two title with a four-point win over Laois.

The All-Ireland Championship started fairly slowly too. They got one back on Limerick, but only thanks to some wasteful shooting from the

Treaty County in the last game at the Gaelic Grounds before its redevelopment. Cork dumped them out of Munster in the semi-final after a replay in what was a difficult week for the county.

The Kingdom had asked for a postponement of that replay after the sad death of Micheál Ó Sé, brother of manager Páidí and father of players Darragh, Tomás and Marc. The game went ahead, however, as Cork's dual commitments made rescheduling difficult.

All three brothers lined out at Páirc Uí Chaoimh on an emotionally charged night, but at the end of it all, Kerry had been consigned to the Qualifiers.

From there though they built up the steam that would see them enter the 2002 All-Ireland final with Sam in their sights.

The goals were flying, nine in all, as they dispatched Wicklow, Fermanagh and Kildare. A slight 19-year-old by the name of Colm Cooper looked increasingly like the superstar he would soon become with each passing challenge.

The Gooch added another four points as Galway were swatted aside in the All-Ireland quarter-final and clocked up 1-5 as Kerry hit 3-19 in a stunning semi-final performance against old rivals Cork – 'orgasmic football', according to Pat Spillane.

They were hitting their stride and they had the added motivation of making up for their humiliating 2001 All-Ireland semi-final loss to Meath. The Royals had won by 15 points, with the 'olés' ringing out 20 minutes from full-time. It was surreal viewing, as the holders were dumped out in embarrassing fashion. When Declan Quill got Kerry's first score of the second half in the 62nd minute, the Meath fans cheered it as if the kicker had been Trevor Giles.

Some knives were sharpened for Páidí Ó Sé after that loss, but in October he was the only name considered for the role. The charismatic Ventry man was subsequently handed a further two-year term.

'For a while there after the Meath game, I went into the bunker that Bin Laden is in,' Ó Sé told Radio Kerry after his reappointment.

That process was designed to draw a line under the Royal debacle, but it could only truly be forgotten by lifting the Sam Maguire in 2002. Few thought they would be denied once they had progressed to the final.

That's not to say that there wasn't some feeling for an Armagh win. In the *Irish Examiner*, journalist Mark Gallagher polled some notable GAA names, with Donegal's Martin McHugh, Dublin's Johnny Magee and Roscommon's Derek Thompson plumping for Kerry. However, Derry's Anthony Tohill said Armagh would win if they stopped Kerry getting a goal or goals, which they did, while Down's Ross Carr provided a firm argument.

'They have an unbelievable focus this year,' said the two-time All-Ireland winner. 'I know some of the boys, and they will give every last breath they have to win the title.'

That focus was crucial as Joe Kernan and his squad tried to wade through the manic euphoria that had gripped the county in the run up to the game.

Months after Armagh ended their 17-year wait for an Ulster title in 1999, a specially commissioned bottle of water went on sale to mark the occasion. Novel as that was, nothing could compare to the build-up to the 2002 final, where anything that could be given an Armagh tint was given an Armagh tint.

CDs were released; orange-and-white paint was daubed over everything from houses to horses. Banners popped up everywhere, stating, 'Thine is the Kingdom, Armagh's is the glory,' and, 'The future's bright, the future's orange,' borrowing the tagline of mobile phone company Orange.

County boundaries didn't provide a release for the players, although the training pitches at the Malachis in Shelagh on the Armagh–Louth border did at least offer some much-needed isolation from the public eye.

'I had gone from working in Armagh to working in Monaghan and there was still no escaping it,' says Oisín McConville. 'I would spend a bit of time in Dundalk, gambling out there, and I got to the stage that I felt I couldn't go anywhere.

'It was a tough time. It was very difficult to get anything done in terms of daily tasks. People were watching training, peering in over the fence. We used the Malachis pitch for a base for a lot of the stuff. Mike Ford, father of George Ford who plays rugby for England, met us at the Malachis. He was flown in from England to take a session on defensive play and movement, but you were always trying to do these things without being seen.

'We used the Malachis and very few knew we were there. It was a brilliant base. That's where we worked on our tactics, because there was a fair degree of paranoia about at that time because people thought we were changing the face of football.'

In Shelagh, a few weeks before the final, Aidan O'Rourke realised that he could never be more ready for a final. When he thinks back to that spell-binding season, it's not the moment the long whistle blew that jumps out. Instead it was tough training sessions all year and in the lead-up to their date with destiny.

'Once we got to the summer months, it was closed off just to us. No one could get there and most people didn't know we were there. It was a great pitch with a top surface, and Shelagh had no underage teams at the time, so it was pretty much ours whenever we wanted it. Handy for Joe, handy for me too.

'I was in the best shape of my life. I was coming out of university football with a good platform to push on, and I worked really hard because I was trying to establish myself.

'We were doing a speed endurance drill at the end of a brutal football session about two weeks out from the All-Ireland final. It was 50 metres there and back, short recovery. John McCloskey was saying before the run, "This is going to give you a window into your conditioning; this will tell you where you're at."

'I blew the field away. There were maybe three sets of eight, and I was winning runs six, seven, eight by maybe ten metres, nobody near me. I got a real confidence from that, because I had to be able to cover the ground; I had to get up and down; I had to be able to keep up with whatever lad was coming at me.

'McCloskey came over to me after and told me I shouldn't have any issues. From that moment on, I just thought, "That's me ready to go."'

As the team departed for Dublin on the night before the game, Joe Kernan and his management team – always the perfectionists – made sure that as many bases as possible were covered.

A plan put together by Hugh Campbell, one of the team's sports psychologists, finally came to fruition.

Campbell had been reading The Fight by Norman Mailer, a book about the famous 'Rumble in the Jungle' between Muhammad Ali and George Foreman. Like millions around the world, the Belfast man was inspired by the Louisville Lip. He wondered how he could channel some of Ali's magic into the Armagh team.

Through a neighbour who was a TV producer, Campbell got a contact for Ali's business organisation. He arranged for one of the greatest sporting stars of all time to write a letter to the team.

On the morning of the final, every player woke up to a letter signed by Ali that said:

'It is with great pleasure that I write to each one of you today, wishing you the best of luck at the All-Ireland Championship final. You have already made history and should be very proud of yourself.

'I understand how much this match means to you, and am honoured if I have provided some inspiration to you along the way. But you are also an inspiration, to the thousands of people who will be watching you, and who have followed the Armagh team all season.

'As one who also has heritage from Ireland (my great grandfather, Abe O'Grady, was an Irish emigrant), I know that "the luck of the Irish" is not just a saying! Best wishes to you on a successful match.

'Your co-countryman, Muhammad Ali.'

The motivation assault continued, as the team were shown a video of the speech 'Peace by Inches' from the film Any Given Sunday.

In this monologue, Al Pacino motivates his American football team by talking about the struggles of life and how the little things – the inches – can make all the difference there, and also on the field.

'You know, when you get old in life, things get taken from you. I mean that's part of life. But you only learn that when you start losing stuff. You find out life's this game of inches. So is football.

'Because in either game, life or football, the margin for error is so small. I mean one half a step too late, or too early, and you don't quite make it. One half-second too slow, too fast, you don't quite catch it.

'The inches we need are everywhere around us. They're in every break of the game, every minute, every second.

'On this team, we fight for that inch. On this team, we tear ourselves and everyone else around us to pieces for that inch. We claw with our fingernails for that inch, because we know when we add up all those inches that's going to make the fucking difference between winning and losing! Between living and dying.'

The original version of the video would have stirred the players, but instead of Pacino delivering the words, it was the Armagh players' families. No shortage of eyes turned watery in that room.

Emotional engine full, the players made their way to Croke Park in that optimal of mental states – inspired but relaxed.

The Armagh fans applauded them as the bus came through the traffic. Unsurprisingly, the Ulster supporters heavily outnumbered their Munster counterparts.

Tickets had been like gold dust. One young fan who had followed them all year couldn't get one anywhere, and in the last roll of the dice he approached a turnstile operator on Hill 16 and said his younger brother was playing in the half-time game. The man laughed, but the inventiveness of the story struck a chord and the fan reached his friends on the terrace just as the teams were parading.

Paul McGrane, who was always serious on the pitch, shared a joke with Benny Tierney before the team photo. Aidan O'Rourke, who had been known to fall asleep before big games, could have easily shut his eyes. Ronan Clarke, as he did before most big games, did throw up though, so nerves weren't entirely absent.

When Kieran McGeeney delivered the final words in the pre-match huddle, Joe Kernan, Paul Grimley and John McCloskey were invited in to complete the circle.

That inspirational message was heeded by Andrew McCann. Knowing that Armagh needed to make use of a favourable breeze in the first half, he got forward inside 30 seconds. He kicked a bad wide, but made up for it with another probing run in the next play that allowed Stevie McDonnell to open the scoring.

The Killeavy man grabbed his second point soon after, following an equaliser by Mike Frank Russell, so often the scourge of the Orchard, at the Hill end. When Ronan Clarke boomed over, Kernan's side were on their way, or so they thought.

That start was a rare bright spot in a half absolutely dominated by the Kingdom. Many of the 2002 squad have never watched the full final back; if they ever get around to it, they'll probably be taken aback by how one-sided that opening period was.

Darragh Ó Sé was Kerry's big name in the middle of the park, but Donal Daly would outshine him as well as Paul McGrane and John Toal in those first 35 minutes. Kerry had settled after their slow start. Enda McNulty's fingertips just stopped Colm Cooper getting in on goal from Sean O'Sullivan's pass, but Kerry were ramping things up and starting to find their range.

When John McEntee was replaced by Barry O'Hagan, minutes after kicking a fine effort despite being concussed, Kerry were 0-8 to 0-5 in front.

The Kingdom kept coming. Russell added a white flag that would have been green only for a deflection off Kieran McGeeney. After Diarmaid Marsden opened his account for the day, Eoin Brosnan scythed through the Orchard defence. Perhaps taken aback by the space afforded to him, he pulled his effort just the wrong side of Benny Tierney's post. Colm Cooper was presented with another sight at goal as the interval approached, but his shot had too much height. Kerry moved into a 0-11 to 0-6 lead.

Armagh's bright start felt like a lifetime ago, and the absence of John McEntee saw the half-forward line lose its shape. The dangerous full-forward unit were too isolated, with Kerry able to cut out the long ball deliveries coming from deep.

One of those half-forwards, Paddy McKeever, was instrumental though as Armagh were handed an invitation back into the game with seconds left in the first half. He sped past John Sheehan after a clever feint and played the ball to Barry O'Hagan. The Clan na nGael man played a one-two with the best man at his wedding, Diarmaid Marsden, before passing across goal to Oisín McConville.

As the Crossmaglen man tried to get his strike off, Declan O'Keefe met him and wrapped his feet around him, dragging him to the ground. John Bannon stretched his arms out wide. Penalty.

How's this for a dose of history? The penalty kick was created in Armagh. Pele, Maradona, Messi – their scoring histories all owe something to the Orchard County. William McCrum was the man responsible, back in 1890, and a statue marks the spot in Milford where he invented it.

Armagh fans may have been inclined to pull it down, given their luck with the spot kick over the years. In 1953, Bill McCorry missed a penalty in Armagh's All-Ireland final loss to Kerry. Paddy Moriarty, who did convert one penalty on the day, joined that unfortunate list in the 1977 final loss to Dublin.

Now, in 2002, Oisín McConville was added to that regrettable list. His strike was clean enough but O'Keefe, who had advanced off his line, got down well to his right and deflected the ball away.

'You think you've lost the All-Ireland for your county. People never believe me when I say this, but I was thinking about Bill McCorry in that moment,' McConville says. 'I had grown up listening to that story, so how could I not? That's all I had known. Bill McCorry was associated with one thing, and that was missing that penalty. That was unfortunate, because if you delve deeper into it, he was a phenomenal footballer. Say Bill McCorry though and that's what people think of, and I thought I was the next one.'

Kerry tried to maximise the damage before half-time, but were met with firm resistance. Diarmaid Marsden barrelled Liam Hassett into touch. Paul McGrane got a super hand in to dispossess Darragh Ó Sé. Aidan O'Rourke and Kieran McGeeney sandwiched Hassett and forced him to overcarry.

Most crucially of all, Marsden picked up the ball and slotted over in the last play of the half. Kerry 0-11 Armagh 0-7.

Before the game on RTÉ, pundit Colm O'Rourke had said that Marsden 'really has let Armagh down in a lot of games', but his teammates and fans certainly didn't see it that way.

As McConville jogged off crestfallen, the damage repair would begin. Ronan Clarke, who wouldn't turn 20 for another 13 days, put the arm around him and patted him on the head.

Inside the dressing room, Kernan once again looked for visual inspiration.

Eamon Mackle, liaison officer and team fixer, was a keen medal collector and included in his haul was a 1934 Armagh county medal won by a Young Irelands side featuring his father, Dan.

One day, he spent a significant amount of money on a batch of six medals, amongst which was a Celtic Cross from Wexford's 1916 All-Ireland triumph.

As the Armagh players sat with their heads bowed in the dressing room, Kernan started the recovery process with a few words. Then he went to his bag of treats and pulled out the plaque he had received for finishing second to Dublin in the 1977 All-Ireland race.

In that moment, it served no purpose other than to remind him he was a loser.

'Do you want one of these?' he asked, before smashing it into pieces against the wall.

'Or do you want one of these?' producing the winning medal that Mackle had snagged at an auction.

Shoulders that had been slumped were soon raised. Eyes looking for the floor started searching out teammates, fists being pumped. 'We can do this,' those reassuring glances said.

Kieran McGeeney's message to his troops was clear. The whole situation wasn't good enough, but he couldn't stomach that the Kerry players were sauntering around Croke Park without a glove being laid on them. Paul Grimley reiterated the point – 'get tight, get tight; let them know they're in a game.'

While belief was being restored to the Armagh players, the 'Sunday Game' studio was having none of it. They got wind of Kernan's plan with the medals, but they saw no turnaround in sight.

'I saw Gerry Adams in the crowd there in his orange colours, surprise, surprise, and he could have told the Armagh full-back line, "Your problems haven't gone away you know,"' said Colm O'Rourke.

'I swear to God, my mother would be faster than most of those three fellas and she has a bit of arthritis in the knee,' said Pat Spillane. It wasn't the first time the Kerry legend had sniped at the Ulster champions, with the full-back line of the McNulty brothers and Francie Bellew usually the main targets.

In the aftermath of the final, a letter was placed into a post box in Armagh simply marked 'Pat the bollocks, Kerry'. It duly arrived at Spillane's door.

Spillane's comments resonated, and they upset some of the Armagh players, according to Justin McNulty.

'It registered with me big time; it made me very angry. It made me very animated and it made me very determined. I thought, "I'll show that bastard. I'll show that fucking bastard." That's what he was to me, talking about amateur sportsmen like that, giving their last breath to be as good as we can be.

'For him to come out and mock us was wrong, simply wrong. It certainly drove me and Enda on, and I'm sure it drove Francie on too.'

Back down below the Hogan Stand, one last important bit of advice was being dished out. Des Jennings, who looked after the mental side of things along with Hugh Campbell, took Oisín McConville aside and told him to go down and kick the ball over the bar when running back onto the pitch.

McConville didn't want to do that because he felt the Kerry fans on the Hill would laugh at him, but when Armagh re-entered the field – after keeping Kerry waiting for several minutes – he blasted a ball down the pitch. He immediately felt as though a weight had been lifted from his shoulders.

The Crossmaglen man's public persona at the time was usually defined in one of two words, depending on how you felt about him – confident or arrogant. He may have appeared to be the last person that mental drills would work on, but he was always open to them, even the extravagant ones created by his former trainer John Morrison.

'I remember one day with the U21s, John had a table, a chair, a stool, a saucer, a cup and a spoon stacked up, and he told us we were the spoons. For things to happen he was telling us that we had to be the ones to stir the cup.

'It was a bit of craic. It was a good way to take away the nerves. I don't know if it was designed around that, but if it was it was brilliant. We played very well that day. I think we might have beaten Tyrone.'

Armagh were notably more physical at the start of the second half. Within a minute, Aidan O'Rourke was booked for laying down a marker on Colm Cooper.

'It certainly wasn't pre-ordained, but at half-time, there was a sense that they were getting too much space and getting away from us,' O'Rourke says of his hit on Cooper.

'Grimbo had given us a blast about not sticking, not being tight enough and letting them slip a yard off. Geezer reinforced that before we went back out. We were both in the toilet just before we went back out and Geezer said, "We need to get some contact on these boys."

'That's as far as it went, but it was in my head that whenever Gooch released a hand pass and was going on for the return, I was following through. It was just a front shoulder. I got a yellow. It's hard to know if it rattled him, but I hurt him when hitting him.

'He hadn't a great second half – I'm not putting it down to that, but it was part of an overall urgency to be more physical and give them less space.'

As well as getting more physical with the Kingdom forwards, John Toal and especially Paul McGrane were starting to wrest control back in midfield.

'McGrane had a huge impact on the second half; the man is a fucking monster,' was Aidan O'Rourke's take.

Marsden opened the second half with a point before Dara Ó Cinnéide and Oisín McConville traded frees off the deck. The Armagh fans had been oddly subdued to that point, but McConville's score brought them to life.

The work of O'Rourke and Kieran McGeeney, who was now in a state of frenzy, in that third quarter was extraordinary. They forced a series of turnovers with tough, well-timed tackling and hits. Liam Hassett's point in the 50th minute really was to be admired, given that he found the range with a manic McGeeney hunting him down.

That was Kerry's 13th point. Amazingly, they would only add one more.

Armagh would post 1-3 in that time, despite O'Rourke and Marsden butchering a golden goal chance before their scoring spree began.

McConville landed a '45' before Ó Cinnéide replied via the same method. The Kerry man was initially stopped in his tracks by a stunning McGeeney block as he tried to flash the ball across goal. With 53:39 on the clock and Kerry ahead 0-14 to 0-10, nobody in Croke Park would have believed that it would be the Kingdom's last score.

It was from Ó Cinnéide's converted '45' that the game, and the history of Armagh football, changed forever. What followed was a team move that will live long in the memory of Orchard fans.

Benny Tierney found Marsden along the Hogan Stand sideline with his restart and the Lurgan man fisted on towards the advancing Andy McCann. The Portadown defender was bottled up but still had the ability to offload to McConville, who took off like a hare.

The Crossmaglen man fisted towards Paul McGrane, but a simple pass was poorly delivered.

'I don't normally fist it with my left. I don't know where that came from;

I'd never do that. That's probably why it was as poor as it was and it put McGrane in trouble.'

McGrane reacted perfectly – rather than try to collect possession, he punched it back into McConville's path and the ace attacker was away.

'McGrane gets himself out of trouble with his intelligence and after that I was comfortable enough,' McConville continues. 'There were no nerves. O'Keefe made the finish handy enough for me, thank fuck. He owed me one, because he saved a big chance from me in 2000.'

The ball was placed low to the near corner. Mayhem in the stands. The man holding his head in his hands after missing the penalty had vanished. This is the McConville the fans love, arms outstretched as he soaks in the adulation from a packed Hill 16.

'People always ask what you remember from the final. What I remember is that they were bringing the Sam Maguire from down below up to the stand just as Oisín was putting the ball in the net,' says Shane Smyth, who watched on from the Armagh bench.

There was still a job to be done though – Kerry were still a point ahead.

After McConville, McDonnell and Barry O'Hagan wasted chances, it was the youngster Ronan Clarke who took care of that, as he turned Seamus Moynihan inside out before curling over.

When asked why they weren't able to get the team over the line in the pursuit of Sam whereas Joe Kernan was able to, former joint-managers Brian Canavan and Brian McAlinden both responded with the same two words: Ronan Clarke.

In the 62nd minute, Aidan O'Rourke and Barry O'Hagan played a one-two that extended to a three-four. At the end of their combination, the ball was with O'Rourke and as he came through midfield, he played the most delicate, dissecting punt pass imaginable. Stevie McDonnell was well covered by two Kerry defenders, but the ball took them both out and bounced into his hands.

McDonnell turned and kicked the ball over the bar. It was the score that won the 2002 All-Ireland final for Armagh.

For ten minutes, Kerry huffed and puffed, but they couldn't find that equalising score. The crescendo of whistles was deafening as Tomás Ó Sé rolled the dice one last time 74 minutes in, but Justin McNulty cut out his forward pass. The ball was worked to Kieran McGeeney and John Bannon blew his whistle.

Armagh were All-Ireland champions for the first time. Dreams do come true.

The first few pitch invaders were bear-hugged away by stewards, but it was an exercise in futility. In 1977, after the semi-final win over Roscommon, the pitch was flooded with fans seconds after the final whistle. Clones had seen its fair share of Armagh breaches in recent times too. It took a bit longer this time, but they were never going to be held back here.

Reactions differed too. After hugging family members and his backroom team, manager Joe Kernan was presented with an unexpected opportunity at retaliation.

'There was a man who criticised Francie the whole year; he was from the Moy direction. For some reason, when the final whistle went, I was hugging Geezer and when I turned around, who was running to hug me only the guy that shit on Francie all year. I drew back across him and I pushed him across the chest and I said, "You'll not fucking slag Francie Bellew now." He was the wrong man at the wrong time.'

Benny Tierney didn't usually feel comfortable with so many people on top of him, but the cameras did capture his moment of joy.

'I'm not great with crowds. I wanted to get off, I wanted to get away. There's a picture of me with the hands up. I think it was on the *Sunday Independent* the next day. I was crying and holding my hands up; I must have gotten it sent to me a thousand times from people since.'

After the full-time analysis from an emotional Jimmy Smyth, one of the heroes of 1977, the camera cut back to the BBC studio. Presenter Jerome Quinn and pundit Martin McHugh were sitting beside an empty chair.

That belonged to Jarlath Burns, who, at the end of the game, had ripped his microphone off his shirt and raced out to the box in front of the studio to celebrate wildly with family and friends. Their coverage of the day would sign off with him singing 'The Boys from the County Armagh'.

'I wasn't aware that the camera was on me at that stage,' says Burns.

'It was into the last five and you were sitting out watching the match and then you have to come in. The sound man comes in and puts on your mic and then the floor manager asks you for a "one, two", a bit of sound.

'The boys were all preparing, as they should be, for a television programme to go out. I was burning up inside. All my dreams. Armagh winning an All-Ireland and a united Ireland are the theme music of your life. One of those was being fulfilled to my right, but I still wasn't sure.

'The final whistle went and we knew we still had five minutes, because Mark Sidebottom was on the pitch. The boys were chatting about what we were going to pick up, and I could not concentrate. My words were, "Fuck this, lads, I'm away."

'I took the microphone off and everyone saw what I did. I couldn't contain my sheer joy at what Armagh had done.'

Brian Canavan was also around the press area that day. The first person to reach over and shake his hand was Pat Spillane.

Those still in the stands looked down at a sea of orange on the Croke Park pitch, as Kieran McGeeney prepared to become the first Armagh man to lift the Sam Maguire. That crowd incursion had caused some practical issues for the players.

'I struggled to get to the presentation. I think Francie was beside me at the start and there was a bit of hugging, I saw someone and I was trying to get to them,' says Aidan O'Rourke. 'Then I realised, I'm 70 yards away, and then I met people I knew and it was all congrats – you couldn't pass, you didn't want to be a dick, but you're thinking you need to get closer.

'Within 30 yards, you couldn't get past, I had to start shouting, "I'm a player, I'm a player." There was a Garda cordon, but I just got there in time, I had 30 seconds to spare.'

Shane Smyth was another who got trapped in the crowd. He was consigned to missing out when he felt two firm hands grabbing him and dragging him past people. Smyth's feet nearly left the ground as he was pulled to the steps of the Hogan and pushed through the barrier of stewards and Guards. When he turned around to see who his saviour had been, he saw one of the Grimley twins. He's still unsure to this day whether it was Mark or John.

Kieran McGeeney, fingers bandaged together, scars of battle evident, picked up the Sam Maguire and looked out on his adoring public. Orange was the colour and, after years of blood, sweat and tears, chasing the seemingly impossible, Armagh were added to the roll of honour.

Back in the changing room, like Burns up in the press area above them, the entire squad and officials linked arms and sang 'The Boys from the County Armagh'.

Sometime later, when the two teams and families were in the players' lounge, Justin McNulty and Kieran McGeeney decided to sneak away for five minutes. As children in Mullaghbawn they had run about together, and they backed each other on every step of the journey to the ultimate goal.

They came out of the players' lounge, down the steps and walked onto the Croke Park pitch, the scene of unbridled happiness a few hours earlier. Content smiles on their faces, they started to walk around for one last chance to feel that famous grass under their feet. A few steps later, two stewards approached them and told them to get off the pitch. A Celtic Cross can open a lot of doors, but not all.

Soon the team departed for the City West, which was also manic for the winners' banquet. While hundreds of fans milled about the Dublin hotel, the Armagh squad retreated to a private bar where they took in what had just been achieved. A few of the greatest hours of their lives.

Even in the pandemonium, the small touches that Kernan always employed were evident. A bus had been arranged to bring wives and partners to the City West, with the players following separately. In their rooms, the suits for the gala dinner were already hanging up by the time they arrived.

When the players finally made it to the banquet, later than anticipated after making the most of their private bar, they were treated like heroes as the team and guests tucked into a dinner of vegetable soup, roast beef and tiramisu. Their lives would never be the same again. Armagh would never be looked at the same way again.

The party went long into the night and heads were sore the next morning as preparations were made for the homecoming.

When the bus pulled out of the City West after another ferocious reception from Armagh fans, the first period of tranquillity arrived. Players passed around the Monday newspapers and read the ratings from the big day; others chatted; some just looked out the window as the bus started to snail north towards the Carrickdale Hotel, the crossing point for Sam Maguire's first visit to Armagh.

At the Carrickdale, where so many of the players had availed of the leisure and gym facilities over the years, cars were backed all the way up to the nearby village of Jonesboro.

Many of the Armagh men had got stronger at the 'Dale, but the south Armagh boys had also spent many a night getting drunk at its famed disco, Laceys. It was a place they all knew well, though none were aware that you could get out onto the roof as they had to on that particular Monday, the crowd simply too big.

The journey of celebration continued on the big yellow Chambers bus. Huge crowds turned out in Crossmaglen and Armagh. In Lurgan the streets were jammed for a bus parade. It was overwhelming and surreal, but this was a day so many supporters never expected to ever arrive.

When the team arrived at the GOAL Challenge match in Crossmaglen on the following Wednesday, Kieran McGeeney carried the Sam Maguire out with the pain of three days' drinking written on his face.

For the next few months, right up until the county awards at the end of January 2003, the players were hostages to the public. They brought the cups back to their clubs; many called into the houses of elderly people unable to join in the celebrations. Dinner dance invites arrived at an astonishing rate. People who said they would die happy if Armagh won the Sam Maguire had seen part of their lives' dreams fulfilled.

Legends were born on 22 September 2002. A 17th team was added to the Sam Maguire roll of honour. Armagh, All-Ireland champions.

Chapter Eleven

A Red Hand Rivalry

Forty-three metres from the Hill 16 goal, Tyrone's Enda McGinley steps inside Armagh defender Andy McCann and takes aim with his right foot ...

Armagh came back to Crossmaglen on the Wednesday after the 2002 All-Ireland final, to face Louth in the GOAL charity game. Ulster broadcaster Adrian Logan was providing colour commentary for the huge crowd of 13,000 at Oliver Plunkett Park.

A Dungannon native, his tongue was firmly in his cheek when he interrupted proceedings with a weather report:

'A deep depression has settled over Tyrone.'

It predictably provoked a laugh and a cheer; spirits were high around the border town, even if the weariness of three days' drinking told on the faces of the Armagh players.

Pat Spillane had said that his mother could outrun the Armagh full-back line. This was now put to the test, as Francie Bellew, Justin McNulty and Enda McNulty took off against a man in a Kerry jersey, blonde wig and suspenders, holding a sign saying 'Spillane's Ma'.

All a bit surreal; all a lot of fun. The party was continuing and Armagh were on top of the world.

The following October, it was neighbours Tyrone's turn to enjoy the occasion, as they celebrated their inaugural All-Ireland success with a fun-filled GOAL game against Monaghan.

What's more, they defeated the Orchard County in the final. Those fans laughing in Crossmaglen in 2002 had had the smiles firmly wiped off their faces.

Losing to your bitter rivals on the biggest stage of all hurt and hurt bad. The manner of the defeat, most notably the controversial dismissal of Diarmaid Marsden after a confrontation with Red Hand wing-back Philip Jordan, made it near impossible to stomach.

Armagh's run to the 2003 All-Ireland final always carried with it the whiff of a hangover from the year before. There was no shortage of character or quality in Joe Kernan's side, but it was hard to shake the sense that not everything was flowing as it had the year before.

Hard evidence appeared in Clones on 11 May 2003, when the reigning Ulster and All-Ireland champions were swatted aside by lowly Monaghan. It was, in fact, their fifth straight loss, having been bettered in the three National League games heading into the summer as well as a play-off game against Laois.

Enda McGinley's shot falls short and lands in the hands of Armagh goal-keeper Paul Hearty ...

That seemed inconceivable, given how they had opened their campaign at Croke Park against Dublin.

In the counties' last League meeting in November 1999, Dublin had sauntered to a 0-14 to 0-6 win. Eight Armagh players who had lined out that day were also in the first 15 for the 2003 clash.

The landscape was different now though. Armagh had conquered their demons on the way to their own version of Nirvana. Any talk of a Croke Park hoodoo had long since lost its voice.

Armagh's All-Ireland celebrations had all been put into cold storage with the presentation of their Celtic Cross medals a few nights before the Dublin League match. Joe Kernan's side were intent on delivering the message that they were not going to be 'one and done'. They certainly did that under lights in front a massive crowd of 54,432.

After a lacklustre 20 minutes from both sides, the champions moved up a gear and took control of every area of the pitch. The 1-15 to 0-7 scoreline told its own story and once Barry Duffy punched home the only goal of the game early in the second half, Armagh were in cruise control.

A heavy pitch in Cross saw them struggle to victory against Cork next time out, before Justin McNulty demonstrated why he was occasionally deployed at full-forward in training under Brian McAlinden and Brian Canavan. He scored the second goal in a good win over Donegal.

Roscommon came to Crossmaglen and left conquered, as the winning streak stretched to four games in the League.

Forewarned is meant to be forearmed, but the wake-up call from Tyrone in round five wouldn't be heeded later in the season.

In November 2002, the Ulster Herald broke the news that Tyrone officials would be meeting a few hours after publication to ratify Mickey Harte as the new Red Hand manager.

Journalist Nigel McDonagh reported that Harte had come out on top of an application process that also saw entries from Brian McIver, Liam Donnelly, Peter Doherty and Eugene McKenna – a sour footnote to the end of his second spell as joint-manager.

McKenna and Art McRory had initially been granted another year after their National League triumph in 2002. However, when McRory was unable to commit, Tyrone deemed the post vacant and McKenna was forced to reapply – unsuccessfully – as a sole candidate.

Paul Hearty fists the ball out to the unmarked Philip Loughran ...

'I don't think the county board come out of it with much credit,' Peter Canavan said the day after Mickey Harte's appointment.

Canavan's ire was directed at the process, not the man chosen. There is every possibility that, had that unexpected diversion not been put in place, the entire Tyrone story would have been very different.

The previous year had been a tough one for Canavan. League success and the introduction of young Minor and U21 All-Ireland winners had pointed to brighter things, but by the time the summer rolled around, the 31-year-old was on the cusp of jacking it in after their shock Qualifier loss to Sligo.

The old failings remained and he looked like he was about to be added to one of the most demoralising lists a player can find himself on – the best GAA players never to win an All-Ireland.

He knew one thing though: Harte was a winner. He had guided the Red Hand County to a Minor All-Ireland and a further two at U21 level.

Who better to guide those players as they attempted to break into the senior ranks?

Three days after Harte's ratification, the pair linked up as Errigal Ciaran earned a super Ulster Club saga win over Crossmaglen. Two games had failed to separate the famous clubs, but with Harte masterminding things from the sideline and Canavan putting on a tour de force performance in attack, they overcame a difficult start to secure a final berth.

Errigal knocked out another All-Ireland champion in the next round as Andy Merrigan holders Ballinderry were dismissed, before getting the better of Enniskillen Gaels in the final.

In late February, Nemo Rangers edged them out in the All-Ireland semi-final, but Canavan didn't endure a restless winter spent stewing on whether or not to play on. He had been active, playing well and, with Harte in his ear, he wasn't going to throw in the towel yet.

The small, consequential details continued to build up. Had Errigal won that semi-final, Canavan would not have featured against Armagh two weeks later.

Philip Loughran clips a simple ball towards Barry O'Hagan in midfield ...

Armagh lost, as God, as Canavan is known in Tyrone, scored three points and claimed a brilliant assist for Owen Mulligan's goal in the 1-9 to 0-10 win. It was only Armagh's second defeat in 11 months, the first of which carried no weight as a second string side lost a McKenna Cup semi-final to Monaghan. More would quickly follow though.

Not many visitors to Crossmaglen left with victories at that time, but Galway did. This was the day when the host club opened the new 1,200-seater Cardinal Ó Fiaich stand – named after a man who had fought so hard for the club's survival during British intimidation and attempted occupation.

Joe Kernan's side signed off with a 1-13 to 2-8 loss in Tralee, but Kerry would need another couple of goals if they were to dislodge Armagh from the knock-out spots. A two-point loss down in the Kingdom wasn't particular concerning, especially as Kieran McGeeney had been sent off with 20 minutes remaining and Marc Ó Sé had won the game with a late, late goal.

The real warning shot came in the Division One semi-final against Laois.

The previous year, Armagh had stormed through the League, but they completely misfired in their four-point Division Two semi-final loss to Laois. Kernan and the Orchard management were fit to be tied by the performance. Although the margin of defeat was down to three points in 2003, the mood wasn't any better as new Laois manager Mick O'Dwyer saw another final arrive on the horizon.

Armagh had just returned from a training camp in England, and Kernan had laid out the importance of the fixture. 'Lads are playing for their places on the team to face Monaghan in the championship on May 11,' he told the *Irish Independent*.

Martin O'Rourke goaled, as he had done in Kerry a few weeks earlier, but not many others put their hands up on a day when McGeeney, Ronan Clarke and Oisín McConville missed out through injury.

Barry O'Hagan, Kieran Hughes and Enda McNulty had been added to the injury list following the Croke Park fixture. Those of a more cynical persuasion believed that Armagh were happy to avoid a final with Tyrone, given that the Red Hands were always guaranteed to get past Fermanagh in the other semi-final.

'Sometimes your pride has to be hurt to get you going again,' opined Kernan.

Barry O'Hagan quickly moves the ball forward to Paul McGrane ...

And Armagh were due to get going again at Clones against a Monaghan team that was game but limited. The Ulster champions were rated 1/7 with the bookies, only to find themselves the victims of an ambush.

Farney boss Colm Coyle had taken a leaf out of Armagh's 2002 play-book, taking the side to Portugal for a training camp in the lead-up to the game.

Paul Finlay was one of four Championship debutants for Monaghan, alongside Vinny Corey, James Coyle and Damien McKenna. Son of Monaghan legend Kieran Finlay, he carried a big reputation with him, having helped Sligo IT to a Sigerson in 2001. Three days before the Armagh game, he was named the Ulster Writers' Player of the Month as the county's U21s made it to the Ulster final.

His inspired form continued at St Tiernach's Park. Damien Freeman was sent off early in the second half for the underdogs, but with Finlay nailing any free that came his way, Monaghan won 0-13 to 0-9.

The Monaghan players celebrated wildly on the pitch. The pub-laden streets around the ground, so often the venue for post-match victory pints for Armagh fans, belonged to Monaghan this time around.

'We had prepared really, really well, and nobody gave us a chance obviously,' says Finlay. 'That meant that there was no pressure on us; there was no pressure on me. It was just go out and try and implement our plan, work our socks off and make it difficult for Armagh. I had one of those bizarre days where everything I kicked just seemed to sail over the bar.'

The defeat was a gut punch for goalkeeper Paul Hearty, who had replaced the retiring Benny Tierney. The Crossmaglen man was starting to think that fate was working against him again.

In 1996 he was his club's goalkeeper as they claimed the Armagh title, but a broken leg sustained in a car accident kept him out of their Ulster campaign. He was fit for the All-Ireland series in 1997, but Joe Kernan, his manager at the time, kept faith with Jarlath McConville as the south Armagh club claimed their first All-Ireland title.

When Kernan did likewise with his county in 2002, Hearty was still left to rue an injury.

He had been the previous management's preferred choice for the 2001 season, but Kernan talked Benny Tierney out of retirement for the 2002 campaign. With the competitive action on the horizon, it still wasn't clear who Kernan would put his trust in.

'At the start of the year, Joe said he'd play us game about in the League and whoever came out on top would be the goalkeeper. The first game was against Louth in Carrickcruppen and I was to play the following week against Wicklow in Aughrim.

'We were training in Davitt Park in Lurgan and we were just doing shots at goal at the end of the session. I went to dive for a ball, turned and landed on my left shoulder. I knew as soon as I landed it was bad.

'I dislocated the shoulder and that was it for eight weeks. I was fit to be back for London, the second-last game. I played over there, but that was the last I played that year unfortunately. I knew early on that I wasn't going to start in the Championship, because I hadn't played all year, so it was probably a little bit different to what happened with Cross.

'It was similar though in that I knew Joe wasn't going to change a winning team. It's a weird emotion there, because unless Benny gets injured you're not going to play, and you don't want anyone getting injured. Benny had a good year and had done very well.

'It still was a bit bittersweet, because I was playing the year before and I was thinking, "This is it, this is me now."

'You would have far rather played of course, but you had to be a sub, work hard and push Benny in every training session and at every game. I felt I did that. I felt that with me breathing down his neck, it made him a better 'keeper, and that's what you want.'

Now Hearty was fit and ready, and with Tierney sailing off to the sunset with his Celtic Cross secure, he was the clear first choice – but any chance of emulating his former colleague would now require a Qualifier run.

Paul McGrane fists with his left hand to clubmate Paddy McKeever ...

While Armagh players have admitted that the early fixtures failed to get pulses racing, they did provide a good breeding ground for getting confidence back into the attack.

Waterford provided a guard of honour at Walsh Park and spent the next 70 minutes admiring the All-Ireland champions too as Man of the Match Stevie McDonnell grabbed 1-4 from play and Oisín McConville ended up with 1-7 in a 19-point win. The Crossmaglen man joined Kieran McGeeney and Ronan Clarke in returning to the first 15.

Antrim in Casement was a sleepy struggle, but that man McDonnell was top dog once again. His half-a-dozen scores were critical in a 0-15 to 0-12 win.

Armagh looked rudderless, badly missing the spark to ignite their season. In short, they were flat. A regular experience for many sporting champions, as the transition from hunters to hunted can be hard to reconcile.

That spark came in the form of the draw for the third round of the 2003 All-Ireland Qualifiers. They were paired with Dublin, the side they had edged out in an epic 2002 semi-final. It was the hardest option available to them, but one that was met with a clenched fist.

There would be no orange invasion of Hill 16 this time, as tickets for the terrace only went on sale two days before the game. Construction staff battled against high winds to quickly remove the stage erected for the Special Olympics closing ceremony.

A crowd of 54,432 had come to Croke Park for their National League meeting earlier in the season, and another 8,711 was added to the attendance for this fixture.

The champions were idling. Could they refute suggestions they were not the team of 2002? Emphatically so. Crucially, that answer came just as they found themselves on the ropes with the referee checking their legs.

The second half was just a few minutes old when Paddy McKeever swung a punch at Darren Homan and was sent off. At that time, Dublin led 0-8 to 0-4.

Four minutes later, it was 14-a-side, as Stephen Cluxton kicked out petulantly at Stevie McDonnell. With the teams back on an even keel numerically, Armagh took absolute control of the content.

Sub goalkeeper Brian Murphy came on, and the hitherto solid Johnny Magee was sacrificed by Tommy Lyons. Armagh grew when his presence down the centre disappeared. Homan too had to depart in the 42nd minute, with a shoulder injury. He had been ruling the roost in midfield until that point.

The McEntee twins were central to Armagh's resurgence, and Joe Kernan chalks this up as possibly Tony's best display in an orange jersey.

'He gave an exhibition. He ploughed through them, took the hits, won the ball, laid it off. He could give the hits too. When you saw Tony Mac lining up the shoulder you knew someone was in trouble,' says Kernan.

From McKeever's sending off, Armagh outscored the Dubs by eight points, to win 0-15 to 0-11. Any questions about the holder's hunger disappeared and Limerick were lambs to the slaughter in the next round.

Through the thunder and lightning and the torrential rain at Dr Hyde Park, McDonnell's relentless march towards the Player of the Year award gathered more pace, with a fantastic 3-4 haul. The Beach Boys were performing at the Roscommon venue the following week, but for now it was 'Shoot Steve E', rather than 'Sloop John B'.

'Listen, I had a fantastic season and I was delighted and honoured to be awarded, but I would give it back in a heartbeat for that second All-Ireland, even the chance to play it again and redeem ourselves,' McDonnell ruefully admits.

Paddy McKeever returns the ball to Barry O'Hagan in midfield ...

The Limerick win set up an All-Ireland quarter-final with Laois, the Leinster champions. Mick O'Dwyer's side had already beaten them in the Division One semi-final. Like the Dublin fixture, this match would require Kernan's men to dig in.

That became clear after just 18 seconds, as Brian 'Beano' McDonald peeled off Enda McNulty, took possession and swung the ball confidently between the sticks.

Both sides had goal chances early on. First, Ian Fitzgerald's daisy-cutter went just the wrong side of Paul Hearty's right-hand post; then Diarmaid Marsden's fierce effort was repelled by Fergal Bryon. The O'Moore goalkeeper would repeat the trick against Stevie McDonnell in the 16th minute.

The sides were level at the break, 0-7 to 0-7. Armagh left plenty of points out there, but the standard of their scoring was exceptional.

Oisín McConville had clipped over from an impossible angle and Aidan O'Rourke kicked a beauty with the outside of his boot. John McEntee landed one from downtown before Marsden danced through a couple of tackles to create space for another score.

Andrew McCann landed another top effort to open the scoring after the interval; Marsden was on target with another great effort after a smart give-and-go with Ronan Clarke; and Philip Loughran floated over a sky-scraper from the sideline.

The quality was evident, but they simply could not shake off Laois. With ten minutes left, the sides were level.

Armagh now found that extra gear though, as they had done against Dublin, and rattled off four points without reply. Laois fought on gamely, but it wasn't enough. Full-time: Armagh 0-15 Laois 0-13.

The Orchard were back in the semi-final for the fourth time in five years. Their clash with Donegal would be a historic one, the first time two Ulster counties had met at that stage.

An all-Ulster final was also guaranteed, as Tyrone had booked a final spot in notorious fashion after a 0-13 to 0-6 win over Kerry the week before.

In that one game, Mickey Harte's side altered the perception of how Gaelic football could be played, and they did it in the face of extreme criticism. Pat Spillane's description of 'puke football' really captured the mood of those outraged by what they were watching.

Spillane has since said that he went too far with the description, and that he had been shaken by seeing an Ulster team coming to Croke Park to play Kerry and not standing back and admiring them.

Tyrone certainly didn't do that – they hunted in packs, forcing Kerry players down empty cul-de-sacs at every available opportunity.

One incredible passage of play from the first half would become immortalised, to be shown countless times in the years since as the relentlessness of the Red Hands stunned the Kingdom.

Sean O'Sullivan clipped a ball down the Hogan Stand side for Dara Ó Cinnéide. The An Ghaeltacht man had barely caught the ball when Gavin Devlin was over the back of him, forcing him to the ground. Kevin Hughes, Philly Jordan and Owen Mulligan quickly converged on the Kerry man, arms regularly stretching out wide to show referee John Bannon that they weren't fouling.

Ó Cinnéide managed to get the ball back towards O'Sullivan. It bounced about, and Ó Cinnéide – a glutton for punishment, obviously – picked up the ball and was again pummelled by four Tyrone players, Sean Cavanagh now in to assist Hughes, Devlin and Mulligan.

Somehow the Kerry man escaped, but Stevie O'Neill was on the scene and had lined him up for a shoulder. Ó Cinnéide took it well, sending the Tyrone man back a yard to allow him to offload to Eoin Brosnan.

The midfielder tried to punch a hole and move forward, but tackles from three players knocked him off balance before Mulligan finished the job with a well-timed shoulder. When Brosnan hit the deck there were an incredible six Tyrone shirts crouched above him. One of those, O'Neill, snuck in and stole the ball and offloaded to Enda McGinley.

The Errigal Ciaran man made a break for it, but was superbly dispossessed by Darragh Ó Sé. Ó Sé then sent Kevin Hughes backwards with a shoulder and side-stepped O'Neill, before four more Tyrone players came in and forced the ball out of his hand.

Ó Sé had no option but to boot the ball forward to the waiting Brian Dooher, who was fouled by John Sheehan.

This whole sequence had taken just 46 seconds, but people watched with jaws on the floor. That sort of intensity had never been seen in such close proximity. Kerry had no answer. Would Armagh? This was the question on everyone's lips, given how strongly they were favoured to take care of Donegal.

Aidan O'Rourke, now an All-Star, tried to temper those expectations in the *Sunday Independent*, saying that Adrian Sweeney was the best forward in the country.

'To be honest, I had more people trying to tap me up for the tickets for the final than I have had for the Donegal game. If the players were to have that same kind of complacency, it would be absolutely suicidal.'

Armagh's desire to be the first team since Cork in 1989 and 1990 to go back-to-back was unquestionable.

Barry O'Hagan looks towards the Canal End goal, bounces the ball and puts his foot through it ...

In January after their All-Ireland win, they were treated to a team holiday in Mauritius. Relaxation was the objective, with only two light sessions booked in on the trip. Management, however, noticed that instead of swim shorts, the players were donning gym shorts. In the end, they trained every day anyway.

Given that they were also the holders, the favourites' tag was completely understandable. But Donegal were emerging from a difficult year, on and off the pitch, to put a memorable run together.

As they looked ahead to the new season, county chairman Danny Harkin suffered a vote of no confidence for his public support of the new Gaelic Players Association. Two months later, Harkin lost out to Brian McEniff for the chairman post.

It was a busy period for McEniff, who had led the county to All-Ireland glory in 1992. He had been on the selection committee to find Mickey Moran's successor, but the panel were repeatedly knocked back. McEniff visited the Donegal players to inform them that the selection committee was struggling, and they asked him to take on the job himself for a year. He accepted.

On the pitch, things had been equally as rocky. Their Division 1A campaign saw the Tír Chonaill side finish dead last, with just one win in seven games – Brendan Devenney hitting 1-6 against Roscommon to secure the county's first competitive victory since their Qualifier win over Meath in July 2002.

When Fermanagh held them to 0-6 in their Ulster quarter-final, Donegal's season looked like it would be drawing to a close soon.

However, with Sweeney hitting top form, they earned Qualifier wins over Longford, Sligo, Tipperary and Down to reach the All-Ireland stage.

That set up a quarter-final clash with Galway. Despite being huge underdogs, they raced into a 0-7 to 0-2 lead, before being caught at the finish, with a second outing needed.

Kevin Walsh's late equaliser for the Tribesmen mattered little though. In the replay, Barry Monaghan produced a heroic effort to curtail Pádraic Joyce, while Sweeney and Devenney dove-tailed beautifully for a brilliant 0-14 to 0-11 win in Castlebar.

Now Armagh were next in the Tír Chonaill rebuilding process, and the shock of the summer nearly came to pass.

If it had, Joe Kernan's side could have blamed nobody but themselves. Over the 70 minutes plus change, Donegal kicked three wides. Armagh had an extraordinary 21. On top of these, they dropped a number of efforts short, hit the crossbar and also the post.

A dozen of those Armagh misses arrived in the first half, a period that started with a light-hearted moment as Stevie McDonnell and Donegal goalkeeper Tony Blake got in each other's faces before the latter put his arms around his opponent and the pair had a little waltz.

That inaccuracy in front of goal meant that even though Armagh had dominated the opening half, they trailed 1-4 to 0-4 as the sides switched ends. Christy Toye had grabbed the goal just before the break, finishing a fine team move with an emphatic low finish past Hearty.

This was Armagh's seventh game of the 2003 championship, but it was the first time they had conceded a goal. It would be the only time.

Just like he had done after Oisín McConville's penalty miss in the 2002 All-Ireland final, it was Diarmaid Marsden who helped calm Armagh down, grabbing a crucial point with the final play of the first half.

Pitchside at the break, Jim Carney, the very first presenter of 'The Sunday Game', found two notable interviewees.

Shay Given, then of Newcastle United in the Premier League, was smiling a lot more than he had the day before, when the Magpies lost out to Birmingham City. This was his first visit to Croke Park since Donegal's 1992 All-Ireland final win over Dublin, and he was dreaming of another trip a few weeks later.

Also giving a few words was Tyrone manager Mickey Harte, who was there to find out who they would be facing in the All-Ireland final. The Red Hand boss made reference to Marsden once again stepping up when the Orchard needed him most.

The big moments went the way of Armagh in the second half too, affording them the opportunity to defend their title against Harte's charges.

Donegal had been first out of the tunnel for the second period, but to the shock of many, Armagh were only 30 seconds behind them. Having left Kerry waiting in the 2002 final after the break, it had become a regular feature for Joe Kernan's side. In the quarter-final against Laois, they took so long that they were booed back onto the pitch by the O'Moore County fans.

The Tír Chonaill men stretched their lead to four points at the start of the second period, but the half was just minutes old when Raymond Sweeney dragged down Oisín McConville. Having also been booked in the 16th minute, this meant that Donegal would play the rest of the game a man down. As an emotional Sweeney tried to make sense of the situation in the tunnel, one man went to comfort him – future Donegal manager Jim McGuinness.

Despite their numerical advantage and complete control of the ball, however, Armagh simply couldn't shake off their Ulster rivals. The yips in front of goal were keeping Donegal in the game.

With 14 minutes left on the clock, Armagh trailed 1-7 to 0-7 when John McEntee launched the ball towards the Hill 16 end. There, Stevie McDonnell, who was not at his cold-blooded best in front of the posts that day, fielded brilliantly above Niall McCready, took a step to his left and finished low past Tony Blake.

A superb Paddy McKeever free put Armagh in front for the first time in the 64th minute, but Adrian Sweeney levelled matters again as the clock ticked into the red.

It was still anyone's game at that stage, but in the end it would be Armagh's. Philip Loughran, the midfielder who had added attacking verve to the side in 2003, fisted over.

Donegal pushed forward, but another man who had broken into the side, Andy Mallon, got an important hand in and Armagh were able to counter at speed. Once again, John McEntee passed forward, and this time Paddy McKeever was free. The Ballyhegan man took a hit from Blake and clipped the ball home. Diarmaid Marsden ran to the crowd celebrating.

Through the noise, however, Michael Monahan's whistle was missed to signal that a penalty had already been awarded.

One point up with four minutes elapsed of a scheduled additional five would see most players tapping over the bar. Not Oisín McConville though. He was never going to give up the chance to bury some penalty demons from the 2002 final. Ruthlessly he blasted to the corner to make it 2-10 to 1-9. Armagh were back in the All-Ireland final.

The fact that Armagh did not play well in the 2003 final against Tyrone did not overly concern Joe Kernan. The result was all that mattered, and it read Tyrone 0-12 Armagh 0-9.

'That was who we were. You can play bad and still win, and it's all about winning,' he says.

Kernan is correct. Armagh, just like his Crossmaglen team, had the knack of grinding out results when things were not going their way. However, in the 2003 All-Ireland final, against their bitter rivals at the time, they were unable to do so. Tyrone claimed their first-ever All-Ireland crown and Peter Canavan would finally be rewarded for those years leaving audiences entranced.

That it was a poor final mattered not one jot to Tyrone fans. The 21 points scored across the game was the lowest tally since Cork beat Meath 0-11 to 0-9 in 1990, but the prize would have been the same had Harte's side won 5-12 to 5-9.

Stevie McDonnell rises high above Cormac McAnallen and Sean Cavanagh, breaking the ball down to Tony McEntee ...

It was a game remembered for two key moments, both of which went against Armagh.

In the 25th minute, Diarmaid Marsden went off the field of play after picking up a head injury. He returned early in the second half, a white patch marking where he had been stitched up after taking a boot to the head, and the first opportunity he got, he put the ball over the bar. Tyrone 0-9 Armagh 0-7.

His day would sour from there.

What happened in the 56th minute of the 2003 All-Ireland final has become the subject of conflicting opinions for all of the main parties involved.

With Armagh attacking, Paddy McKeever fouled the ball and Brian White blew for a free out. The TV cameras focussed on McKeever as Sean Cavanagh raised a fist and celebrated in his face, before Ryan McMenamin came in to have a few words.

Off camera, Philip Jordan lay on the ground as a number of players engaged in a wrestling match. White consulted with his umpire, marched out the field, scribbled in his book and produced a red card.

Without argument, Marsden started the slow walk to the sideline. Tyrone defender Conor Gormley clapped him on his way before giving him a consoling pat on the back – the Carrickmore man seeming to instantly realise his applauding had appeared as bad sportsmanship – before Stevie McDonnell had a few words with the departing player.

The footage was, and remains, unclear. A high view caught the incident and it shows Marsden and Gormley engaged in a bit of shoving before Jordan points and makes a beeline straight towards the Armagh player. When he arrives, he tries to push Marsden, whose left arm does come up. Whether he strikes, or even attempts to strike, probably comes down to whether your flag is orange and white or red and white.

Marsden was exonerated three months later by the GAA's Central Council. Armagh were disgusted that the Games Administration Council didn't clear Marsden a month earlier after reviewing video footage, and would not rest on the matter.

That they eventually got the red card overturned on a technicality did little to quell the tribalism that surrounded supporters' views on the situation. Two decades on, the incident still rankles with quite a few of the Armagh panel, but the degree of anger varies considerably.

The two men involved, who haven't crossed paths since that day, still have differing accounts of what happened.

'Everyone from Armagh, 99 per cent of them anyway, will have one opinion on what happened, and that will be that I dived to get Diarmaid sent off,' says Jordan. 'There's no guilt on my part in terms of what happened. When you have a camera angle that doesn't show what actually happened, then it's very easy for people to say what happened.

'My intentions were to shove Diarmaid for a prior incident [with Conor Gormley]. Ultimately I am not going to say whether he deserved to be sent off or not, but the one thing I can say for sure is that I didn't dive.'

Marsden, and Armagh, would argue the toss on that.

'It was really, really hard to take at the time,' Marsden says. 'It was the biggest day of the year and it ended like that. It was tough to get over that. If we hadn't have won in 2002, it would have been much, much worse.

'The circumstances of that day, there is nothing you can do about it now. The appeal was won on a technicality. It wasn't people in a room looking at a video and saying you didn't deserve to get sent off, and that leaves it a bit unfinished from my perspective. It leaves a bit of a sour taste.

'I know in my own heart what happened.'

Tony McEntee shakes off a Gavin Devlin challenge and passes to Stevie McDonnell ...

Armagh half-back Aidan O'Rourke is certainly on the lower end of the scale when it comes to ill-will towards Jordan, despite being one of Marsden's biggest admirers. What's more, he felt that the red card shouldn't have had much of an impact on the game.

'I didn't blame Jordan. If you're telling me a Tyrone man had to do that for them to win the All-Ireland, I wouldn't expect him to do anything else. That's just the game. It's not about the Corinthian spirit – it's about whatever the fuck needs done. Yeah, he over-egged it; yeah, he engineered it probably with his antagonism.

'Did Diarmaid deserve to be sent off? I'd say no. In the moment it didn't really matter to me. The task was still the same; we were still trying to find a few holes in those boys to create a few scores. That's what we couldn't do; we had loads of ball, but couldn't score.'

One ball, one potential score, stood out more than any.

Stevie McDonnell is clean through on goal ...

... and with the net about to bulge, Tyrone defender Conor Gormley comes from nowhere to execute the most famous block in GAA history.

When McDonnell eyed up John Devine in the 68th minute of the final, Tyrone led 0-11 to 0-8. If Joe Kernan could have picked one player to be on the end of that move, it would have been the Killeavy man.

Nobody inside that stadium expected anything other than to see the net ripple – nobody except Gormley, of course. Naturally, he earned the nickname Block in the aftermath.

So would McDonnell do anything differently if he had the opportunity again?

'Absolutely. I always say that it was a block worthy of winning any All-Ireland final. If Enda McNulty or Andy Mallon had pulled off that block, we'd be applauding them.

'I didn't see him, it was a block out of nowhere. If I had caught Conor Gormley out of the corner of my eye, I would have tried to cut inside him. He would have had no option but to pull me down. The likelihood is that we would have had a penalty and a possible goal out of it.

'I was pulling the trigger because I thought I had a clear route to goal. Who's to say that the shot would have rattled the net? Ifs and buts; however, given the form I was in, you would have expected it to be a goal. If I could turn back the clock, I would have taken a look over the right shoulder and had a check; I probably would have fashioned a more central shot.

'I've never been blocked like that again.'

Oisín McConville did eat into Tyrone's lead, but Stevie O'Neill landed the clincher for Tyrone.

No back-to-back for Armagh. The sea of orange from 2002 replaced by red and white. The first all-Ulster All-Ireland final had gone the way of Tyrone.

As the jubilant Tyrone players climbed the Hogan Cup steps to watch Peter Canavan's history-making moment, Kieran McGeeney stood in the Hogan Stand tunnel. Right shoulder against the wall, no tears, but dejection was clearly painted across his face. He stood there to soak in that pain. To bank it for the future.

Chapter Twelve

The Pursuit of Greatness

Joe Kernan would remain in charge of Armagh for another four seasons after the 2003 All-Ireland final defeat. That entire period seemed defined by one saying:

'I remember telling guys, "Good teams win one; great teams win two," and that's a massive regret, that we didn't get the second,' says Kernan.

'The fact that they were there four or five years may have taken an edge off what they had for those latter stages. They were going a long time playing high tempo matches. Winning Ulsters and then losing three years in a row to teams that would win the All-Ireland takes its toll. Could I say that at the time? No. You maybe lose that wee fraction and that's all it takes.

'You need that wee fraction to win an All-Ireland, and it just takes that wee fraction to lose one too. That's life. A wise man told me a long time ago that you should be thankful for what you have and not what you think you should have.'

Armagh's 2002 squad can be thankful for their Celtic Cross, but those wise words will not convince all of them that they shouldn't have had more.

That the Orchard County didn't win a second All-Ireland is a travesty. That they didn't play in another final after 2003 is simply astonishing.

The 2004 National League campaign pointed to a team still in shock from the previous September. Kernan had tried to freshen things up with an infusion of youth. Players like Brian Mallon, JP Donnelly, Paul Watters, Barry Shannon, Stephen Kernan, Malachy Mackin and Oliver 'Ozzie' Gaughran were all given chances to shine, but the team was still mostly made up of All-Ireland winners.

Despite that, Galway beat them by eight points, while Cavan put 3-12 past them in a 13-point victory. Limerick beat the Orchard 0-15 to 0-12 as they just about avoided the drop to Division 2B.

The match with the Breffni County was played in a sombre atmosphere. The teams wore black armbands, in tribute to Tyrone player Cormac McAnallen, who had died five days earlier. The Orchard squad had provided a guard of honour at his funeral a few days earlier, just months after they had battled it out in the All-Ireland final at Croke Park.

While the 2004 National League had been a struggle for Armagh, the Ulster Championship fixture list provided that one ingredient that all managers love – motivation. Armagh were down to face a Monaghan side that had dumped them out so dramatically in 2003 and had celebrated so vociferously.

The Orchard squad had also revisited La Manga in the lead-up to the game, in an attempt to rediscover some of their 2002 mojo.

Kieran McGeeney passed a late fitness test, but stayed on the sidelines throughout, such was the ease of the victory over the Farney County. The team sheet had shown two changes in all from the '03 All-Ireland final, with Paddy McKeever and Martin O'Rourke coming in for McGeeney and John McEntee. McKeever and O'Rourke both featured on the scoreboard, as did the other four listed forwards, in a 2-19 to 0-10 win.

Cavan were up next, and Armagh were expected to make up for their trimming a few months earlier in the League. The game was defined by an incident in the very first minute.

The St Michael's, Enniskillen, band was still walking around the outside of the pitch when Pierce McKenna raised his arm and struck out at Francie Bellew. Referee Michael Monahan was left with little choice but to issue a red card, while Breffni fans were furious with Bellew's reaction as he lay prone on the floor.

Despite being massive underdogs and having to play with a man less for 69 minutes in the baking heat, Cavan came at Kernan's side like wolves. With eight minutes left, incredibly, they were two points to the good.

Armagh's bench was stacked though. Diarmaid Marsden came on and kicked a point and then Brian Mallon entered the fray, scoring two points. Kernan's men nabbed the final four scores, to win 0-15 to 0-13.

The Orchard manager went to watch the other semi-final, between Donegal and All-Ireland holders Tyrone, a week later. He left five minutes early, with the game already over as a contest, but nobody would have predicted before the match that Donegal would be in the ascendancy.

For the first time since Casement Park in Belfast hosted the thrilling 1971 Ulster final between Down and Derry, won 4-15 to 4-11 by the Mourne County, the provincial decider was taken away from Clones. When the Ulster Council opted for Croke Park, to deal with demand, they knew that criticism would come their way. And it certainly did, but the fact that 67,136 fans came through the turnstiles justified their call. It would stay there for the following two seasons too, as interest in Ulster football reached an all-time high.

While the occasion for that 2004 final was special, the competitiveness of the game didn't match it. Armagh produced some scintillating football to win out 3-15 to 0-11. Marsden flicked home the first goal. Paddy McKeever finished beautifully after a nice one-two with Stevie McDonnell, and Oisín McConville also raised a green flag.

Kieran McGeeney, collecting the Anglo Celt jointly with Paul McGrane, was stony-faced when making the speech, the pained expression he had worn watching Tyrone hoist aloft the Sam Maguire the year before still evident in his features.

With 2003 Player of the Year Stevie McDonnell starting to get back into the groove, Armagh looked capable of redemption in the All-Ireland series.

It had been a busy summer for McDonnell off the pitch too. After Club Energise Sport was launched in 2003, they produced a football and hurling advert that featured some of the country's top stars playing on a lake. In the football version, McDonnell was handed the headline role, blasting the ball to the net. His profile was bringing plenty of attention.

'An Adidas deal was there for me. There were other sponsorship opportunities too,' he says. 'I was lucky, not every player got to get these deals, but I got a lot of those through the GPA. Five or six years after the Club Energise one, Lucozade Sport knocked on the door and I met them. They put an offer on the table.

'When I thought about it, I thought about the GPA and the endorsement deal they had with Club Energise. This was a competitor brand. I told them what I had been offered, so they told me to decline Lucozade Sport and they would get the same offer from Club Energise.

'It was never that hectic or that mad that I'd need an agent, but I was very lucky. There was a lot on the table, but I knew that wasn't going to last forever.'

Back on the pitch, all eyes were now on a potential heavyweight semi-final with Tyrone. On the same quarter-final double-bill at Croke Park, Armagh were expected to steamroll a Fermanagh side that hadn't beaten them in the Championship since 1966. Tyrone were to do likewise against Mayo in the second game. Incredibly, Fermanagh and Mayo would ultimately meet in the semi-final.

The thought of Armagh missing out on a fifth All-Ireland semi-final in six years was almost inconceivable, even though the Erne County had toppled Meath, Cork and Donegal on their journey to the last eight. They also had received a walkover against Tipperary – the Munster men failed to field after their manager Andy Shortall resigned three days before the clash.

However, when Armagh shot into an early 0-5 to 0-1 lead, Fermanagh's summer voyage looked like it had reached its final destination.

Charlie Mulgrew's side hit seven of the next eight points though and, just before the break, received another major boost when Enda McNulty was red-carded.

The Mullaghbawn man could, with real justification, claim to be Ulster's top corner-back at that time. He was one of few to ever play the game that seemed to have the measure of Tyrone legend Peter Canavan. He was experienced, driven and wholly committed, which makes his kamikaze tackle in the 36th minute all the more difficult to understand. As Marty McGrath passed the ball forward, McNulty came in at pace, late, and caught him with his arm. The Fermanagh man's mouth was left crimson as a result.

Armagh's response to going a man down was a positive one. They kicked the first three points of the second period to lead by one, and that was the margin heading into the final ten minutes.

Fermanagh equalised, and the scoreboard operators then had an 11-minute break as the teams entered additional time on level terms.

As the game drifted into its 74th and final minute, Tony McEntee booted the ball forward in an attempt to engineer an Armagh winner, but it landed into the chest of a green jersey. Fermanagh broke up the field at pace and the ball was worked out to the left, where Tom Brewster was on hand to clip over, sparking manic scenes amongst the watching Fermanagh – and Tyrone – fans. When pitch invasions occur after the first game in a double-header, you know something special has happened.

'That was our fault; the heads were obviously turned and we took Fermanagh for granted,' says Joe Kernan. 'Enda did the stupid thing and was sent off. There was no need to foul out there at that time. He was well away from the goal.'

Aidan O'Rourke is in no doubt that Armagh would have won the All-Ireland that year if they hadn't slipped up, but he puts the losing of the game more down to referee John Bannon than McNulty.

'I don't want to sound bitter. John Bannon beat us against Fermanagh; it's black and white. Looking back on the 2002 final, he didn't do us any harm in certain situations, but he had a huge influence on 2004 and I have told him that personally. He worked with myself and Kieran [McGeeney] in Kildare, reffing in-house games. He's a great fella, but he is fallible just like everyone else.

'Fermanagh's game was very like Tyrone's – they defended deep in numbers and had huge pace and energy on the counter. They ran the ball and their wing-forwards drew frees all day; they dived consistently.'

People may debate whether or not Armagh would have completed the job in 2004, but not a sinner in the country would have betted against them lifting Sam Maguire the following year had they not come unstuck against their great rivals, Tyrone.

Three epic games, three different results – but when all was said and done, it was the Red Hands who escaped alive and lifted the All-Ireland for a second time. Plenty of regret – and no shortage of devastation – in the Armagh camp.

Having taken a year out from his job with the Irish Sports Council, Kieran McGeeney spent the early part of 2005 in New Zealand. He travelled, sure, but his main aim was to train like a professional athlete, to ensure that he was in the best physical condition that a Gaelic footballer had perhaps ever been in.

Geezer was always willing to seek that extra edge, not just physically, but mentally too. The themes of a book given to him by Hugh Campbell about the Battle of Thermopylae – later adapted into the Spartan film *300* – always stayed with him.

He knew just how good Armagh were in 2005. Even though bonds between certain players and members of the management team had become slightly strained – a seemingly inevitable consequence of success – McGeeney knew a golden opportunity for that second title, that tag of greatness, was available.

The spring brought silverware. McDonnell kicked half a dozen points from play in the National League semi-final win over Mayo. Joe Kernan's history-making side would create even more when they claimed the county's first-ever National League title.

On a day that saw Monaghan fans invade the pitch after their last-gasp Division Two win over Meath, Stevie from Killeavy saw off four different Wexford defenders to go one better and kick seven from play. Brian Mallon also caught the eye with four points from play, while Paul McCormack, who started the first game of the 2002 Championship campaign, came up from the back to nab a point, but the dual player saw his season's ambitions hampered by a shoulder injury.

Like Monaghan in 2004, an Ulster opener against Fermanagh – conquerors of Armagh the summer before – provided the necessary motivation. Kevin McElvanna stepped in for the suspended Enda McNulty and Armagh sauntered to a 2-12 to 1-7 win, Brian Mallon again catching the eye.

A smouldering, spiteful two-game saga with Donegal, that saw the Tír Chonaill men finish with 12 men in the second game and Armagh with 14 after Francie Bellew was dismissed, ended with Armagh winning by seven points. A blistering 1-3 in six minutes against Derry, John Toal with the goal, set up an Ulster final meeting with Tyrone.

Despite the rivals sharing the Anglo Celt between them since 1999, it would be the first provincial decider between Armagh and Tyrone since the famed Frank McGuigan final of 1984, when the Ardboe maestro finished with 11 points.

Stevie O'Neill tried to pay his own tribute to the Red Hand legend when he got the run on Bellew, as the Tyrone man finished with 10 points, six of those coming from play. Kernan kept Bellew on the attacker for the majority of the game before switching Enda McNulty onto him, but most of the damage was done. Still one point shy of McGuigan though.

There were some other notable moments from that Croke Park clash. Early in the second half, Aaron Kernan was presented with a tap-over free, but mishit it, landing the ball into John Devine's arms. The Tyrone goal-keeper took a step back, and the ball clearly went over the line, only for the umpires to miss it.

Oisín McConville's 44th minute goal, coming after a clean lift off the ground by Stevie McDonnell, was only Armagh's fifth score, and it was keeping them on Tyrone's coat tails. Like McDonnell, McConville lifted the ball clean off the ground, but both fouls went unnoticed by Pat McEnaney.

With a minute of normal time remaining, Kernan's men were four points down. McConville, as so often was his trademark, decided to do something about it. He blasted the ball towards the square, where McDonnell – who had a rare bad day at the office – won it above Shane Sweeney and scrambled the ball under Devine.

There was still time to rescue the situation. McGeeney fielded the ball brilliantly and off-loaded to Paul McGrane, who galloped forward and split the posts with a beautiful floated effort. Armagh's battling qualities had come to the fore once again, and somehow they had secured a replay.

Perhaps the most significant moment from that game was the serious injury picked up by Armagh's warhorse in the middle, John Toal. Minutes before half-time, the Keady player delivered a ball towards the Canal End and was tackled by Stevie O'Neill as he did so. The collision caused catastrophic injuries, but Toal's first thought was, 'How has the ref not given a free where that's landed?'

'It happens,' Toal says. 'Nobody means to hurt anyone. If he had caught me a bit higher or a bit lower, the chances are that you would have bounced up and ran on. Just where I was caught, the damage was done.

'I knew once I was hit that I was in trouble. I had plenty of injuries before and I was able to get through them. I broke my pelvis once and I played on for the rest of the game, but I knew I wasn't getting up this time.'

O'Neill got wind of how bad the injury was and phoned Toal to apologise. He wanted to visit him prior to surgery too, but the Armagh player said that there was no need.

When medical staff examined Toal's knee, they found the sort of injuries that would normally be associated with a car accident. His knee cap was still protecting the blood vessels below, so an amputation was not required.

'I just remember waking up. It was an operation that was supposed to take two or three hours, but it ended up being seven or eight hours,' Toal says. 'It was only when they went in that they realised there was a lot more damage than originally thought. There was a nerve and something else, and if they had been damaged I could have lost my leg or lost the power in my front.'

Toal's place for the replay was taken by Philip Loughran, while Ciaran McKeever also came into the starting line-up, with Tony McEntee dropping out.

Cullyhanna man McKeever had captained the county to their first All-Ireland U21 crown the year before. Some senior players in the changing room were leaning on the management to find a spot for him in the first 15.

That chance came his way in the replay, and he would end up playing his part in one of the most poisonous atmospheres ever experienced at Croke Park.

Something hung in the air that day, a simmering cloud that manifested into nastiness in the stands and tension on the field. As a combative game progressed, some fans from both counties failed to cover themselves in glory as arguments broke out around the ground.

It wasn't much better on the field.

'Do these folk heroes not realise that long after they retire, such behaviour will leave a blot on their characters that will never be erased by Ulster or All-Ireland medals?' asked Offaly 1982 All-Ireland-winning manager Eugene McGee in his *Sunday Independent* column the next day.

Early in the second half, Paul McGrane, who had already been booked, should have been sent off for a closed-fist tackle on the chin of Philip Jordan. The Moy man remembers little of the incident. Referee Michael Collins instead booked Brian Mallon in error.

Cards were being flashed regularly in the second period, with Brian McGuigan, Francie Bellew and McKeever all entering the book.

Armagh in particular looked frustrated. Unlike the drawn game, they had played the better of the two teams, but trailed 0-11 to 0-7 when Mickey Harte tried to seal the deal with a double substitution in the 52nd minute.

Peter Canavan, taken off at half time in the first match due to ongoing issues with his rib and shoulder, was coming on with Owen Mulligan.

Small details can make major impacts. When Canavan came on, the next play was a hop ball. That was won by Kieran McGeeney before Canavan wrapped him up and gave away a foul. A number of Armagh players, particularly Philly Loughran, took exception to this and a shoving match involving 17 players broke out.

A few scores were settled in those seconds, but the most abiding image was Ciaran McKeever reaching into the scrum of bodies and dragging Peter Canavan, whose jersey had ridden up to reveal his black under-armour, across the turf as if he was a bag of cement. Gavin Devlin defended his captain's honour by getting in the Armagh man's face.

Canavan, mere moments after coming on and having failed to touch the ball, was sent off. It was a very harsh call. The Errigal man did not throw a punch in the melee – even if he had wanted to, it would have been impossible with ten bodies lying on top of him. His subsequent appeal was successful.

McKeever followed him to the line as he picked up his second yellow card.

In the 61st minute, Tyrone lost another player, Stevie O'Neill, to a second yellow card. Like Canavan, he ultimately earned a reprieve after Collins later admitted misreading notes, misinterpreting a prior tick for O'Neill as a first yellow card.

In the 71st minute, John McEntee came down the Hogan Stand flank in an attempt to find a winner after Armagh had hit a purple patch to draw level. Ryan McMenamin stopped him in the process with a foul, and then dropped his knee onto McEntee's jaw. Incredibly, the Tyrone player was only booked, and afterwards he phoned McEntee to apologise.

McConville nailed the resulting free to send Armagh into the lead, and the same player stepped up to add the final finishing touch in the 74th minute.

Armagh were Ulster champions for the fifth time in seven years. They had managed just five provincial titles in the 109 years before Jarlath Burns raised the Anglo Celt in 1999.

The win came at a cost though. Ciaran McKeever and Paul McGrane were cited, as was Tyrone's Ryan McMenamin. They were handed proposed four-week bans. After initial appeals were rejected, the two counties pushed it all the way and the trio were free to play.

For Armagh, this meant their pair were available for a comfortable quarter-final win over Laois. With Tyrone responding to their Ulster final replay loss with wins over Monaghan and Dublin – after a replay – the scene was set for the final chapter of the greatest Irish sporting rivalry of the summer.

Thankfully, the ill-will that had enveloped the Ulster final replay appeared to have evaporated in the crowd. Republic of Ireland players Shay Given and Clinton Morrison were amongst those taking this highly anticipated game in, and they were treated to an absolute classic of an All-Ireland semi-final.

For Armagh supporters, two moments in the most heart-breaking of losses will take some time to recover from.

With 71:03 on the clock, and both teams having posted 1-12, Steven O'Neill cut inside Ciaran McKeever and was tugged back. There wasn't much force, but enough for Paddy Russell to award the free.

'The free at the end was heart-breaking, because it was a foul. There was a tug, but sure there were tugs all day. If he'd blown the whistle for full-time, who would have said anything?' says Joe Kernan.

Owen Mulligan and Peter Canavan joked about who was going to take it, and in the end, experience outweighed youthful vigour and Canavan split the posts. Despite one minute and 17 seconds having elapsed between the awarding of the free and Paul Hearty restarting play, Russell blew his full-time whistle as soon as Hearty took the resulting kick-out.

Final score: Tyrone 1-13 Armagh 1-12.

When Mulligan and Canavan were laughing about the free, the RTÉ cameras cut to a helpless-looking Kieran McGeeney. Incredibly, Geezer was watching his dreams go up in smoke for another year from the sidelines rather than in the heat of the battle.

In the 63rd minute, and just after his son Aaron had put Armagh in front, Joe Kernan withdrew McGeeney for Enda McNulty after the Orchard management team had conferred for a few minutes. Exiting, Geezer had a few words with his manager.

Such calls can look either inspired or insipid, depending on what transpires thereafter. At Croke Park, Tyrone kicked three of the last four points to earn a famous victory.

When Canavan's effort sailed over the crossbar, Kernan knew that the knives would be out for withdrawing the team's spiritual leader. While he will always feel that there was justification in the decision, he is big enough to admit that he has made mistakes in this game. Looking back now, the call is a regret, especially as Tyrone players like Sean Cavanagh have since said that it gave them a real boost.

'Do I regret it? Of course I do,' says Kernan. 'I respected Geezer so much, but we were only thinking of one thing, and that was winning the game. Did we nearly win it? We nearly did. Did his coming off cost us? Everyone will have their own idea.'

That Armagh–Tyrone 2005 All-Ireland semi-final was the pinnacle of one of the most captivating rivalries Gaelic football has seen. It gripped not only the two counties, but the entire GAA public. Sparkling football, immense physicality – sometimes overstepping the mark – and a fight to the death every time ensured that the games were essential viewing.

Between 2000 and 2005, the rivals met eight times in Championship football. Tyrone won three, Armagh won three and two were drawn. Tyrone left that period with two Sam Maguire successes to Armagh's one, and the bragging rights belong to them, but both got over the line – and each pushed the other to new heights.

It's not surprising that Armagh were unable to get back to that pinnacle, given what they had put into the game over the previous decade. It was the closest they ever got to realising the greatness they strived so hard for.

In 2006, it looked like they might have got another opening though. That year, an incredible 19,631 rocked up to Belfast to watch Armagh and Tyrone clash in the Dr McKenna Cup semi-final. The Orchard stormed to another Ulster title, and led Kerry by two points at half time in the All-Ireland quarter-final.

'I'll always remember Jack O'Connor saying to me at the 2006 All-Star function how we had ripped Kerry apart in that first half,' says Stevie McDonnell. 'He couldn't figure it out. For ten minutes before half time, he went in behind the Hill goals to watch our movement, and he said he never saw a partnership like it in his life. He said it was telepathic between me and Ronan Clarke.'

In the second half, Kerry let loose. Kieran Donaghy scored a brilliant goal and screamed in the face of Paul Hearty.

In his autobiography What Do You Think of That?, the Kerry attacker claims that Hearty was continually giving him verbals and at one stage said, 'Go on Donaghy, you big soft basketball cry baby.' Hearty said he would buy Donaghy a pint if he ever bumped into him.

Kerry lost Paul Galvin to a red card after he grappled with John Toal. The Keady man, who was on water-carrying duty, landed a stiff right in the ruckus and was also lined.

'Galvin walked past and said a mouthful, but I didn't take much notice,' says Toal. 'Then he put his hand on my chest and nipped me, and I banged his hand down. Next thing he fell onto the ground as if I had hit him. That wasn't a big deal because it didn't matter if I did, because I wasn't a player.

'I don't know why he rolled around to have me sent off. I think he realised that and that's when he got up and grabbed me and pulled me to the line. I went so far and I said I'm going no further.'

At that stage, Kerry's lead was just a goal, but even with an extra man, Armagh couldn't save their season. By the end, the Kingdom had eight points to spare en route to yet another All-Ireland title.

That was their 34th All-Ireland triumph, while Armagh's chances of securing that elusive second title were drifting further away.

2007 saw Kernan's time with his county come to an end. It ended with something of a whimper, given the thunder and noise that had accompanied the previous five seasons.

It hadn't been the easiest of campaigns, with wins rare in the League. At one stage, he had to deal with the absence of 19 players through injury. Ronan Clarke, Francie Bellew, Brian Mallon and JP Donnelly all suffered cruciate injuries.

For the first time on Kernan's watch, the Orchard County failed to win a Championship match, with Donegal and Derry inflicting one-point defeats to end their season. The latter of those also brought about the symbolic end of the side that had made it to the top of the mountain, and possibly left a bit of their souls behind as they tried to rescale it.

The end was quick that season, but no less frustrating.

In Ballybofey, Diarmaid Marsden was making his championship return. He had been talked back into action, having stepped away in March 2005.

Debutant Brendan Donaghy performed really well, while Paul McGrane, Marty O'Rourke – who got into a first-half altercation with his former Dromintee manager Brian McIver – and Aaron Kernan also caught the eye.

The Orchard County were far and away the better side, but there are few things as perilous in Gaelic football than a two-point lead. As the game ticked into its final minute, Brendan Devenney launched an effort towards goal and, under pressure from Kevin Cassidy, Paul Hearty fumbled it to the net.

As frustrating as that loss was, a game with Derry at their favoured venue, Clones, should have started what could have been a productive Qualifier run.

The result appeared preordained, with the embarrassingly low number of Derry fans showing up earning them the nickname The Clones 500. Paddy Crozier's Oakleaf outfit produced the sort of fight not expected of them, and the game hung in the balance in the closing stages.

Armagh were left furious when Paul Keenan was denied what looked like a nailed-on free in the final moments. Derry's Michael McGoldrick then made a great run up the field before setting up Collie Devlin to kick the winner.

Less than two weeks later, Kernan stepped down. Two months after that, Kieran McGeeney retired. He had made his first appearance for the county in 1992.

Armagh would bounce back and win the Ulster title in 2008 under new manager Peter McDonnell, but if that day against Derry, and the parting announcements that followed, felt like the end of an era, it's because it was.

Epilogue

The Little Gold One

Stevie McDonnell is pissed off. He has tried his best, but it seems that some men just want to be cut free from that glorious odyssey of 2002.

Time and time again, McDonnell and a few others have tried to organise reunions and trips away, so that the Armagh players can reminisce and remember. It's always the same faces that are prepared to actually commit.

The team's WhatsApp group had lost participants over the years, but ahead of the 20-year anniversary of that famous September day, those drifters are being added back in. McDonnell is a keen user of Twitter. He can see the Down 1991 and '94 squads regularly meeting for golf days, while that particular Mourne WhatsApp group is always buzzing. Armagh's isn't.

'It's annoying, because when you look back, that was one of the tightest group of players you'd ever come across,' says McDonnell. 'Everyone has their lives to live, but I would always be one for having regular reunions if possible. It's always the same handful of boys that attend those events.

'Some boys don't tend to go for it and it's disappointing, because any time we do get together, it's always great craic. We probably have drifted. We have a WhatsApp group that includes every player, it's a players' one, it doesn't involve management, but some stay on the outskirts. That's part and parcel of retiring and moving away from the game.'

Not many have moved away from the game though. A 2016 study by *Gaelic Life* found that, of the 30 players in the 2002 All-Ireland squad, 25 had moved into coaching, across 'nine counties, 29 clubs, five sports, three continents and two universities'.

Kieran McGeeney (Kildare, Armagh), Aidan O'Rourke (Louth), Tony McEntee (Sligo) and Justin McNulty (Laois) have all managed at senior inter-county level. Paul McCormack (Louth) has managed hurling at senior county level, while Ronan Clarke (Armagh) has been manager at ladies' senior inter-county level. Many more have been involved with county coaching teams.

Whatever they go on to achieve in the game, or indeed in life, those men will collectively be remembered for taking Armagh football to heights previously considered unachievable. They fulfilled dreams of their own, and of the thousands who followed them for decades, from the lowest divisions to the ultimate highs of those spell-binding days, when the stands in Croke Park were given an orange tint.

'It's life-changing stuff,' Justin McNulty remarks. 'You can have all the Ulsters, all the accolades as an individual – All-Stars and Ulster All-Stars

– it all pales into insignificance until you get the little gold one in your pocket.

'I remember the physio Alan Kelly, who would have treated a lot of us down through the years, talking about hurlers. He'd have DJ Carey coming in or Henry Shefflin, that calibre of player. He'd ask them about the little gold one.

'There are so many footballers and hurlers who have received wonderful recognition, but they don't have the little gold one. I am blessed. Through whatever circumstances, a group of players came together at the same time to have the hunger and the desire, the vision and the ambition to do it.

'Many times we couldn't go to training – "Sorry, lads, no training tonight, there has been a murder in Bellaghy, too dangerous." We came through all that, the Troubles in the background, and it's a huge credit to our parents first of all, parents who built the character of the men. Also the teachers and coaches in schools and universities, and the coaches in clubs.

'The fans too – the atmosphere around those games was just extraordinary. I don't remember a bad word ever being said to me throughout my career by an Armagh fan. Not once. They might have thought it, but all I ever got was a pat on the back.

'This is a wonderful, wonderful thing, and I want it to be experienced by as many players as possible. I'm getting teary thinking about it.'

McNulty and Joe Kernan's troops were the team that unscrewed that bottle of whiskey that had sat in McKeever's bar for so long. They were the team that broke through so many barriers.

That little gold one eluded the Orchard County on 99 previous occasions, but the men of 2002 were not to be denied. Armagh: All-Ireland champions.

Great books from

Hundreds of books
for all occasions

From beautiful gifts to books you'll want to keep forever! The best writing, wonderful illustration and leading design.
Discover books for readers of all ages.

Follow us for all the latest news and information, or go to our website to explore our full range of titles.

 TheOBrienPress    TheOBrienPress

 OBrienPress    TheOBrienPress

Visit, explore, buy
obrien.ie